Appliqué

Appliqué

BY EVANGELINE SHEARS
AND DIANTHA FIELDING

WATSON-GUPTILL PUBLICATIONS, NEW YORK
PITMAN PUBLISHING, LONDON

Published 1972 in the U.S.A. and Canada by Watson-Guptill Publications,
a division of Billboard Publications, Inc.,
165 West 46 Street, New York, N.Y.
Published simultaneously in Great Britain by Sir Isaac Pitman & Sons Ltd.,
39 Parker Street, Kingsway, London WC2B 5PB
Manufactured in Japan
First Printing, 1972

Library of Congress Cataloging in Publication Data
Shears, Evangeline.
  Applique.
  Bibliography: p.
  1. Applique. I. Fielding, Diantha, joint author.
II. Title
TT779.S5   746.4'4   75-190520
ISBN 0-8230-0240-3

(U.K.) ISBN 0-273-00049-7

ACKNOWLEDGMENTS

Diantha and Evangeline wish to thank the following for their inspiration and help, in one form or another: Marybelle, Jim, Louise, Russell, Chris, Melissa, Bryce, Tom, Phyllis, Betsy, Brian, Janice, Thor, Paula, Fred, Frank, Ken, Otto, Don, Carolyn, Wally, Jacqueline, Pedro, Judith, Tom, Ro, Van and DeeDee. A special thanks to photographer Bob Lopez for his patience, good humor, and professional ability.

CONTENTS

INTRODUCTION

Appliqué is the attachment of fabric, usually by sewing, to the surface of another piece of fabric. Nearly everyone has the simple tools, materials, and skill necessary for the work: cloth, scissors, needle, thread, and the ability to sew a simple in-and-out running stitch. Basically that's it, yet the medium allows you to be as versatile and creative as your own imagination. With appliqué you can silently communicate your individuality and personal warmth, your own brand of humor; you can express your joys, sorrows, or political opinions; through it you can bring values to your world that a technological society doesn't produce.

Appliqué has a unique dimension and life peculiar to itself. Always, the forms should be strong and clean. The strength and invention of these forms will grow from direct contact with your materials. It takes meticulous work, if done in a craftsmanlike way, but it lends itself to a greater vigor and bursting forth of energies than other more regimented methods of needlework. With the addition of embroidery, the portrayal of detail can become even richer. As your work progresses, you'll find yourself developing a greater capacity for inventiveness and variation. The vocabulary of your forms will change with the excitement engendered by your discoveries.

Fabric has a basic two-dimensional nature. However, the play of light on the surfaces of differing fabrics, and the play of solid appliquéd shapes against the shadows cast by them, as well as the light and shadows created by any quilting techniques, augments this two-dimensional nature with a third—a tactile, sensual, inviting depth.

1
DESIGN SOURCES

Beginners often ask, "Where do you get ideas for designs?" If you feel uncertain about creating designs, you may think you lack the design sense to start from scratch and must settle for copying someone else's appliqué work. However, it's a great waste of time and energy to copy others' work; there isn't much of you in the piece when it's completed. Copied work lacks the vitality of creativity and is a mere finger exercise. Observing the work of others you admire can inspire ideas of your own. But copying a design is a denial of your own creative ability. Appliqué as an art medium is as personally revealing as a tone of voice, and personal involvement is where the fun lies.

SELECTING A DESIGN

A design is essentially a planned arrangement of details to be worked out. Ideas for design come from sources, such as nature, common to all of us. Each individual perceives objects in a different way. One person sees a sunflower as a luxurious burst of golden petals on a sentinel-straight stalk. Another sees it as a swelling orb of burnished seeds, haloed in yellow on a willowy stalk. In your work, you'll automatically emphasize the details that personally appeal to you.

The way you feel about things also influences your design. A favorite color or combination of colors may dictate not only your palette but the subjects you choose as well. For instance, if you're most comfortable with warm, earthy tones you may choose to do dandelions and daisies rather than lupines or lilacs.

Don't worry about being original. You'll create something original without trying because of the way *you* see and feel about your subject and the materials you select to work with. What makes your finished product unique is the expression of your personality in it.

USING SIMPLE SHAPES

Appliqué, with its simple shapes and clean lines, is a strong medium. Bold and direct, it lends itself to simple, straightforward designs, and when these designs are worked in fabric, they have their own added impact. This impact is partially because fabric is being used in an unexpected way, for designs that you're more accustomed to seeing in paintings, prints, and sculpture.

In appliqué, the main point is to keep the shapes simple. What you really want is the essence of the object and not a direct copy with all of its individual details. Think in terms of the overall shape of an object, flattened out and simplified. It may help you to think of geometric shapes—the circle, rectangle, triangle, and square. A house, for instance, might become a rectangle with a triangular-shaped roof and square windows. Close your eyes and try to visualize a particular tree; then draw the remembered shape. What you've drawn is probably close to the idea or concept of your tree and a better, cleaner shape for appliqué than a realistic rendering. Keep in mind that appliqué works best with simple, basic shapes.

DESIGN IDEAS FROM EVERYDAY THINGS

However you spend your day, look around as you go about your activities; the ordinary things hold a major source of design ideas. The bowl full of fruit in the kitchen, stacked vegetables in the market, street signs, telephone poles and interwoven highwires, your children and their toys, family hobbies, pets, the shapes of numerals and letters, for that matter the shapes of words themselves, all translate well into appliqué. Trees, birds, flowers, fruit, insects, clouds, pebbles, the happenstance patterns of cast shadows—nature offers exciting subjects to explore. Most of these things are available to us daily for they clothe our physical world—and they are all design.

DESIGNS FOR SPECIFIC PEOPLE

Take a clue from the special interests of the person the work is intended for—music, surfing, the theater, sports, collections, treehouse building, or whatever. For instance, if you want to make a wall hanging for your son's room, and he spends most of his waking hours under an old car he's building, you'll have no problem in choosing a subject for the design of the wall hanging.

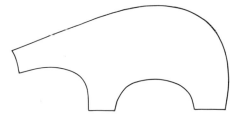

This basic animal shape gives the indication of a body, legs, and head. With slight alterations, you can transform it into all sorts of animals.

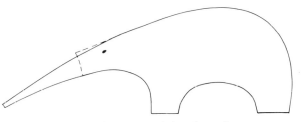

Add an elongated snout, and the shape becomes an anteater.

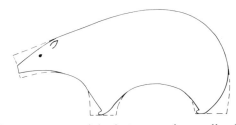

Cut away some of the form to make smaller feet and a tapered head, and you have a grizzly.

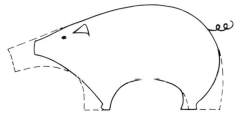

Some of the form is trimmed away to reveal the distinctive head and feet of a pig. The tail might be made by embroidery or a twist of material.

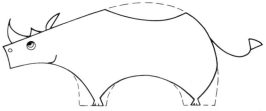

You can construct even the most complicated animals, like this rhinoceros, from the basic shape.

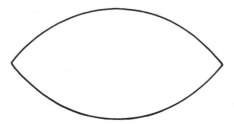

This leaf shape can be used to form animals, plants, and abstract designs.

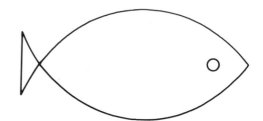

The fish is a simple appliqué form.

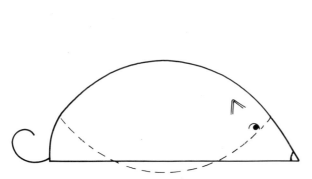

When you make a mouse, note that the tail and nose section of the body do not follow the same gradation of curve as the basic shape. The tail section is pushed in a little, and the nose is stretched out.

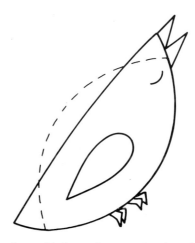

To make a bird nesting, again the shape is extended, and simple indications of body parts are added.

You can add very elaborate feet and tail feathers to this strolling bird, or you can keep them very simple.

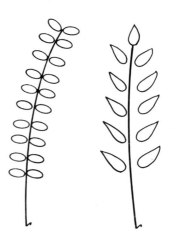

You can group several of the basic shapes together to indicate leaves or branches, altering the shape where you need to.

This design uses the basic shape to suggest a flower.

Here a basic shape is used in several different sizes to create an elaborate rose window design.

You can suggest trees, even specific varieties like this mulberry, by using simple shapes.

You can indicate the trunk of this elm by an appliquéd piece, by an embroidered outline, or by heavy yarn tacked in place.

This stylized shape effectively depicts a weeping willow without working out each individual branch.

Trimmed boxwood trees are especially good subjects for appliqué; they have simple, geometric shapes.

Rimbu Bird (Above) by Lucile Brokaw. 35" x 30". Wild life of the imagination was the source of this fantasy design. The wool and cotton appliqué incorporates yarn-wrapped teeth from a bamboo rake. The head of the bird is assembled from wood and feathers, and the background is linen. This piece is mounted on thin plywood.

Sun Symbol (Right) by Gonzalo Duran. 38½" x 30". Duran has given the sun a friendly, human quality. The piece includes a variety of bright-colored and textured fabrics which have been machine stitched to an upholstery damask background. The added fringe completes the piece, and a wooden rod is used for hanging it.

Landscape *by Esther Feldman. The palisades on the Southern California coast with boats, the setting sun, and various houses were the source of this design. The artist uses appliqué of cotton, wool, lace, and net along with a variety of embroidery stitches.*

Aries *by Lucile Brokaw. Mounted on thin plywood, 32" x 56". A symbol of the zodiac was the basis of this wall hanging. The ram is made of batiklike cotton with leather horns and hoofs. The lines on the horns are embroidered with wool yarn. The background is wool and heavy linen upholstery fabric. All the stitching was done by hand.*

The Banjo Player *by Gonzalo Duran. A western folk music star inspired this lively wall hanging. The appliqué uses lightweight cotton, upholstery fabric, eyelet embroidery, and satin. The artist machine stitched the pieces to a heavy, textured cotton ground fabric. Fringe and pompoms were added, and a metal sword was slipped through the tabs.*

Appliquéd Tent. *Cotton appliqué in navy blue, black, white, red and ochre on a canvas tent, 15' x 30' and 12' high at the center post. This tent was made and appliquéd by Egyptian needleworkers. It is owned by Mr. and Mrs. Pedro Miller of California. Detail at left.*

Cucurucu Palomas *by Lucile Brokaw. Mounted on tempered Masonite. Collection Lamont Johnson. A popular Mexican folk song inspired this stitchery in cotton and wool. "Cucurucu" is the sound the doves make. The eyes, beaks, and feet are hand embroidered with wool yarn.*

Herald Angel *by Diantha Fielding. 8" x 16". The Christmas season inspired this wall hanging. The background is machine embroidered brocade, the wings are upholstery damask, the gown is silk and felt, and the halo is cotton gingham and felt. The artist used a fine-line, black ink pen to draw in details.*

IDEAS FROM BOOKS AND MAGAZINES

It's perfectly all right to translate design from another medium into appliqué. Books are a wonderful source of inspiration for design motifs as well as useful references for details of specific objects. Dictionaries and encyclopedias are the mother lode with their illustrations of things like Montgolfier balloons, floral cross sections, cell structure, the wheels and cogs of mechanical devices, architectural details, musical instruments, ship's rigging, maps, and anatomy. Seed catalogs offer nifty illustrations of the color and structure of specific flowers and vegetables. Legends and fairy tales, histories, heroes, and important events may suggest ideas for you to develop. Your own interpretation of these subjects will be fresh and authentic. The Hampton Court maze or the labyrinth of the legendary minotaur would make a marvelous cut-through reverse appliqué piece (Chapter 9). Looking through books and magazines of all kinds is one of your most fruitful sources of design ideas.

PERSONAL AND FAMILY SYMBOLS

Your personal family history, a sort of visual unwinding of memory spools, offers you design inspiration. A special gift, the flowers in a wedding bouquet, a remembered trip, or any treasured memory of special importance to you is exciting subject matter to develop.

Symbolism is a precise and crystalized means of communicating—an abbreviation for the sake of brevity and to facilitate expression. All the sciences, both ancient and modern, have picturesque code symbols that lend themselves beautifully to appliqué, but developing your own personal symbols for use on a house flag or other personal articles is also challenging.

CLIPPINGS AND SKETCHBOOKS

Start a clipping file of your own for future reference. When you see photographs and illustrations that interest you in magazines, newspapers, or advertising brochures, cut them out and add them to your file.

A sketchbook or note pad carried with you is valuable as an idea source of your own making. Quick sketches, however simple, act as graphic key words, helping you to recall the arrangements and patterns of fleeting designs that appeal to you.

Design is everywhere; it confronts you constantly. As you work, you'll find yourself becoming more and more aware of the power of suggestion which even the most common objects have. Rely on your own feelings and responses to the world about you, and you'll find the ordinary, honest stuff of life re-emerging in your work in fresh and exciting designs.

2
FABRICS AND EQUIPMENT

Most of the basic fabrics and equipment you need for appliqué work can be found in your home. To begin, all you need are sharp scissors with pointed tips, sewing threads in a variety of colors, a thimble, an assortment of needles and pins, and a collection of fabrics. At the end of the chapter you'll find a more detailed list that includes additional materials you may need for special projects.

BUILDING A COLLECTION OF FABRICS

You'll want a collection of fabrics in a variety of colors, prints, and materials: checks, dots, florals, ginghams, plaids, stripes, and as complete a selection of solid color cottons as possible—from dark to light, grayed to bright—as well as textured fabrics in all colors. Compiling such a collection may take some doing at first, but as your work progresses and one project leads to another, your supply of materials will automatically grow.

Since there are few among us brave enough to toss out anything made from cloth that is still usable, you probably already have a start on the collection: out-of-style or outgrown garments (if the fabric is in good condition), the material you picked up to make the skirt you never got around to making, scraps from other sewing projects, and so forth. You can also make a rag run among friends who sew and thereby gather a greater variety. All these become candidates for your work, and the more material you have to choose from, the more inspired you'll be.

Of course, you'll augment this beginning with fabric from yard goods shops. It's only fair to warn you here that while shopping for fabric for a specific project, you'll run across remnants you have no immediate use for but can't live without. Don't worry—they add to your possibilities for future projects, and you will use them. In general, choose fabrics that are colorfast and preshrunk, that don't fray when cut, and that have a hard finish and an even weave.

EASY FABRICS TO USE

Beginners find it easier to use new cotton with a firm weave, such as percale or broadcloth. New cotton has sizing in it, which makes it crisper and therefore easier to work with. But don't discount the use of cherished scraps for the applied shapes. Felt is fine to use for appliqué. It comes in a variety of bright colors; the edges cut cleanly; and you don't have to turn them under. Remember, however, that felt won't wash and must be dry cleaned.

FABRICS TO AVOID
OR USE WITH CARE

Avoid any fabric, such as heavy canvas, that's difficult to get a needle through. Burlap too isn't a satisfactory material for appliqué; it sags, ravels when cut, and has an abrasive quality that makes it uncomfortable to work with. Wool is fine to use for the ground piece, but since it has a lot of natural life and bounce, beginners find it difficult to use for the applied shapes. Linen, too, has a lot of natural resilience that makes it difficult for beginners to use for applied shapes.

SHEARS

A good, sharp pair of dressmaker shears really are a must. Now's the time to invest in a pair if you don't already have them. In addition, a smaller pair of scissors and a pair of embroidery scissors are helpful for cutting small shapes. You know how the man of the house feels about your hammering nails with the handle of a screwdriver? Adopt the same attitude about your tools: let everyone in the family know that your fabric scissors are out of bounds for cutting paper, hangnails, or any other nonfabric material.

THREAD

Cotton-covered Dacron thread and mercerized cotton thread are both good for appliqué. The color of the thread can match, contrast, or blend with the color of the piece you're stitching. Thread color that sharply contrasts with fabric color becomes an additional design element — rather like emphasizing a motif with a dark line. A more subtle contrast, such as purple or green thread on blue fabric of the same value, adds richness and depth. In addition to sewing thread for appliqué work, you'll want a collection of wool yarn and cotton

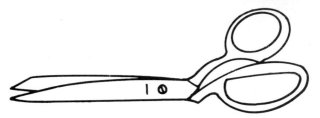

The shape of dressmaker shears allows you to cut fabric without lifting the cloth when you cut around a pattern.

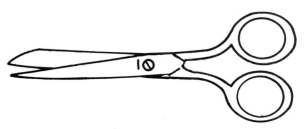

Sewing scissors are a versatile tool with many uses. Notice how their handles and blades differ from dressmaker shears.

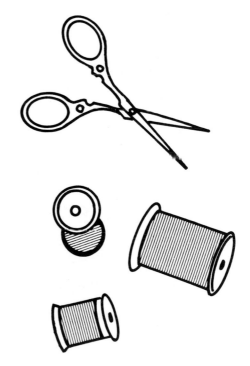

You will also need embroidery scissors, valuable for working with small shapes, and a wide selection of thread.

Use silk dressmaker pins which won't rust or leave marks in the fabric. To keep them from getting lost, stick the pins in a pincushion.

The use of a thimble will speed your work and save your fingers.

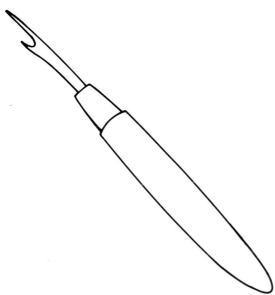

A seam ripper is used for removing basting stitches and turning under seam allowances.

and silk floss for embroidery embellishment. All these threads can be picked up, a few at a time, when you're buying fabric for specific projects. You'll soon have a formidable array of colors and kinds of threads to experiment with.

NEEDLES

One package of regular sewing needles or sharps of assorted sizes and one package of long-eye embroidery needles of assorted sizes will suffice for nearly all your work. For appliqué work, use a needle that sews easily through the fabric you're working with. Generally, the heavier the fabric, the larger the needle, but experiment with several sizes to find out what's most comfortable for you. You'll use embroidery needles to add stitchery embellishment to your design, but many stitchers also use them for appliqué work on heavy or tightly woven fabrics. The large eye makes a larger hole in the fabric than a regular sewing needle, allowing you to pull the thread through more easily.

PINS

You'll need straight pins to position the cut shapes to the ground fabric before you begin stitching. Silk dressmaker pins are good to use because their slender shafts allow them to enter the fabric smoothly and easily without leaving a hole when they're removed.

THIMBLE

If you've never used a thimble, learning to sew with one may seem clumsy and uncomfortable at first. But the proper use of the thimble saves you many sore fingers and results in better, faster work. Usually worn on the middle finger of the right hand, a thimble directs and pushes the needle through the fabric. It's an absolute necessity when you're sewing heavy, closely woven material or several layers of fabric.

NECESSARY MATERIALS

1. Dressmaker shears—4″ to 6″ blades with pointed tips.

2. Straight pins—fine silk pins.

3. Pincushion—a wrist pincushion is the easiest to use.

4. Sewing needles— #5 to #8.

5. Embroidery needles— #3 to #9, large eye.

6. Thimble.

7. Fabrics—cottons, wools, blends, etc.

8. Embroidery hoop—6″ to 8″.

9. Sewing threads—mercerized cotton or cotton-covered Dacron.

10. Embroidery threads—cotton floss and yarns.

11. Paper for drawing designs—drawing pad, butcher paper, or white shelf paper.

12. Soft pencil.

OPTIONAL MATERIALS

1. Sewing scissors.

2. Tracing paper.

3. Seam ripper—helps to turn under allowance.

4. 1″ masking tape.

5. Embroidery scissors.

6. Trimmings—braids, various edgings, beads, etc.

SPECIAL PROJECT MATERIALS

1. White glue for cut-and-paste appliqué.

2. Dowels and finials for hanging banners.

3. Filling for quilt and hotpads—dacron or cotton batting or cotton flannel.

3
BASIC STITCHERY AND APPLIQUÉ TECHNIQUES

Appliqué has a world of potential as a creative medium, and as with all the arts, it too has its disciplines. Skill with the simple tools and techniques of appliqué comes with experience—through experimentation and practice. Nevertheless, the most imaginative design will remain an unfulfilled potential if your work is haphazard. Each project requires awareness, care, and thought, from the planning stage to the last stitch. Possibly the key word is *care;* for when you really care about something, it naturally follows that you put forth your best effort on its behalf. With this attitude you'll develop the pride in your work of the true craftsman.

CHOOSING A PROJECT

Since your beginning projects will be experiments with design and exercises for acquiring skills, it's most important to begin appliquéing something you really want or can use, whether the article is a special-occasion gift for a loved one, something for your home, or something just for you. Your joy and enthusiasm while watching your design emerge with the applied pieces more than compensates for any technique difficulties—all of them solvable—that you may run into.

Also, it's best for beginners to start with small, easy to handle projects such as a cushion cover, a kerchief, or a set of luncheon napkins. With a small project you'll quickly see the results of your efforts and that's encouraging. If your project doesn't work out, little is lost in terms of time or money. But a great deal is gained because you learn as much about what to do and not to do through mistakes as well as success. Even expert stitchers sometimes begin projects they abandon before finishing, and you'll no doubt do the same on occasion.

If you're not satisfied with a piece, put it aside for awhile and start on something else. Perhaps all it needs is incubation time. When you return to it with a fresh eye, you'll probably see what was wrong and how to remedy the problem.

BEGINNING SKETCHES

Once you've decided on a project, begin by making thumbnail sketches on paper until you like what you see and the design seems complete. Then make a full scale drawing of your intended piece; butcher paper or white shelf paper is good for this. If the design isn't as effective full scale as it was in the small drawing, make whatever changes or additions of detail it seems to need. Remember that your drawing is only a useful tool, not an irrevocable commitment.

CHOOSING FABRIC

Now gather a group of fabrics in diverse patterns and colors that please you, even those you doubt will work together. First, choose your ground fabric, the material that will form the background of the design; then work with swatches about the size the applied shapes are to be— selecting and rejecting, changing and moving them around on your drawing till your eye says, "Yes, that's a pleasing balance." Colors and patterns that you thought wouldn't work together sometimes turn out to be an exciting combination. This composing takes time and judgment, but eventually you'll learn to reject a cherished piece of cloth without a qualm. You'll use it in a future project, you know.

TRANSFERRING THE DESIGN

As your skill increases, and therefore your confidence, you'll probably work in a spontaneous manner, cutting fabric shapes freehand. But in the beginning you may feel more secure with a pattern to follow. If so, make a copy of your full scale drawing to use as a blueprint. Cut out the shapes from your first drawing to use as a pattern for cutting the fabric. Cut fabric shapes ¼" larger all around than the pattern; this ¼" provides a margin of material which you can fold underneath to create a smooth edge, the *turnunder allowance*. Use the uncut, full-scale drawing of your design as a guide when you pin the cut shapes to the ground fabric.

It may be helpful to pencil the design lightly on the ground fabric. You can do this most easily by taping the drawing to a sunny window; masking tape is good for this. Then tape the ground fabric over the drawing and trace it lightly with a pencil.

WORKING WITH APPLIQUÉ SHAPES

An applied piece of fabric will lie beautifully flat if it's cut with the straight of its fabric running the same way as the straight of the fabric to which it's applied. The straight of a piece of fabric runs parallel to its selvage edge, but often you work with scraps that have no selvage. When the straight of the goods is not easily discernible to the eye, you can find the straight by pulling a single thread from the cut edge.

Don't iron under the allowance before appliquéing. You'll lose some of the spontaneous look of handwork if everything is pressed flat. If you feel the need, lightly baste under the allowance. Although this isn't necessary, it may help you to place and reposition the shapes to create a more pleasing balance on the ground fabric because your cut shapes are the same size that they'll be on the finished article. It isn't necessary to baste the appliqué shapes to the ground fabric before stitching them down; pinning them is sufficient.

Generally when cutting, pinning, or stitching, work on a smooth, flat surface so that the fabric doesn't bunch or draw. There'll be times when you'll want to study a larger piece vertically while positioning and repositioning your shapes to the ground fabric. To do this, tack the top of the ground piece to a door or pin it to your draperies. But be sure the shapes are smooth and flat before stitching them down.

HOW TO MITER CORNERS

Two of the most awkward things to do well in appliqué are to *miter corners* neatly (making sharp, often square, corners) and to turn sharp inside curves. Practice on scrap fabric first to become familiar with these techniques and thus avoid overhandling a shape when you're working on a project.

There are two methods for making sharp points and square corners. Both methods work equally well, and it's only a matter of which you prefer. Light basting of the shape before appliquéing is helpful to the beginner, but as you become adept, you'll simply turn the corners as you sew.

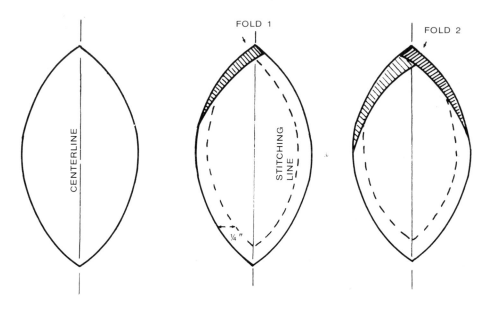

The two fold method requires two folds of the cloth, one on each side of the point.

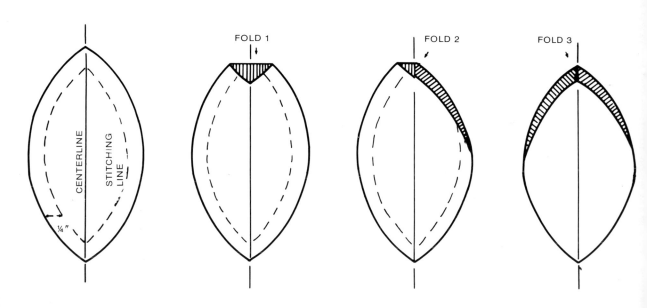

The three fold method uses three folds of the cloth, one at the point and one on each side.

TWO FOLD METHOD

This method of making a sharp point or a square corner requires two folds at the point. Starting on the left side, fold the edge of the cloth over about ¼″ toward the center. Crease the fold firmly between your thumb and forefinger. Then fold the right side over the left and crease the fold firmly.

THREE FOLD METHOD

To make a sharp point or a square corner with this method, you must make three folds at the point. Fold the point straight down about ¼″. Fold in the right side, then the left side so that the edges meet in the center of the shape. Crease the line of fold firmly between your thumb and forefinger.

INSIDE AND OUTSIDE CURVES

To make inside and outside curves you'll generally have to clip the turnunder allowance to prevent distortion of the shape. The sharper the curve, the more numerous and closely spaced your clips must be. To prevent fraying, make the clips no more than two-thirds the depth of the allowance. Simple curved shapes such as leaf shapes, may be cut on the bias; thus eliminating the need to clip.

TURNING UNDER FABRIC WITH A SEAM RIPPER

A seam ripper helps you turn under the allowance of a cut shape as you are working. Turn under a short length of the ¼″ allowance and pin the shape in place on the ground fabric. Insert the longer end of the seam ripper under the piece you're applying, but make sure that the short tooth stays on top of the shape. As you pull the seam ripper toward you, it will turn the allowance under. Pin the shape to the ground fabric as you go.

BASIC STITCHES

If learning to sew a fine seam was part of your early training, well and good—but if not, don't let it worry you. You'll find the two basic stitches most frequently used in appliqué—the *running stitch* and the

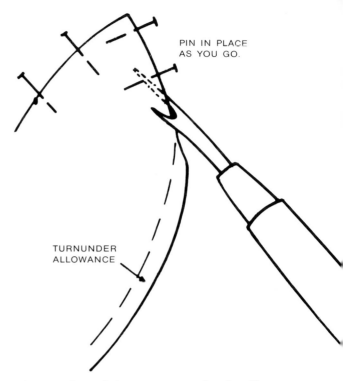

PIN IN PLACE AS YOU GO.

TURNUNDER ALLOWANCE

A seam ripper helps you turn under the allowance of a cut shape. Insert the longer end of the seam ripper's divided points under the cloth and pull the seam ripper toward you. This action will fold under the turnunder allowance, and you can pin the appliqué piece in place as you go.

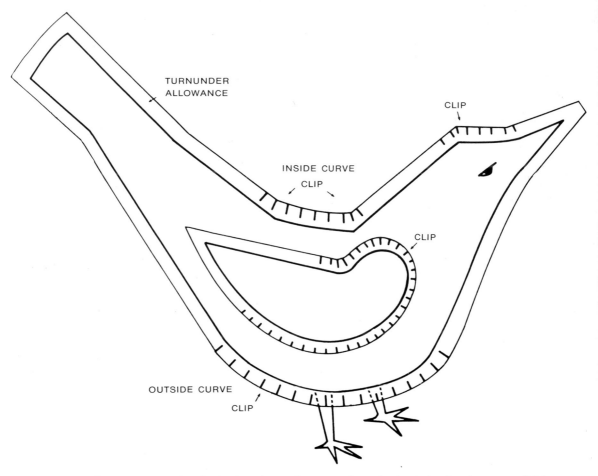

TURNUNDER
ALLOWANCE

CLIP

INSIDE CURVE

CLIP

CLIP

OUTSIDE CURVE

CLIP

This is a pattern for the bird in the Mulberry Bush Quilt, *(p. 84). The short, parallel lines show where you should clip the turnunder allowance to make sharp inside and outside curves.*

slip stitch—simple to master. The important thing to keep in mind is that the stitches should be neat and even. Though the expression of your thoughts and ideas through design is your main concern, if your craftsmanship is shoddy your good idea just won't come off, and you'll really be dissatisfied.

RUNNING STITCH

The running stitch is the one you'll use most often. To start, use a single knotted thread. No more than $\frac{1}{8}''$ from the edge, draw the needle from the underside to the front of the piece to be applied. The knot is then buried under the applied piece. Make the running stitches by weaving the needle point in and out, through the piece you're applying and the ground fabric. You may make the stitches one at a time or weave the needle through the fabric layers several times before pulling it through. For permanent seams make your stitches tiny—$\frac{1}{16}''$ to $\frac{1}{8}''$ long. These stitches show on the surface and become part of the total design. Secure your thread with one or two tiny backstitches (p. 31) on the reverse side of your work.

SLIP STITCH

The slip stitch is almost invisible on the surface of the work and gives the effect of a slightly padded edge. This is a good stitch to use when you don't want stitches to show or when you want a more puffed, rounded edge. Use a single knotted thread in the same color as the piece to be attached. From the inside of the turnunder allowance, draw the needle through the folded edge of the piece you're attaching. Then pick up a thread of the ground fabric at this same point. Reinsert your needle into the fold and come out again about $\frac{1}{8}''$ to $\frac{1}{4}''$ from the first stitch. Continue stitching through the fold, then through the ground fabric. When your sewing is complete, draw the needle through to the back of the ground fabric and take one or two tiny backstitches to secure your thread.

BACKSTITCH

A backstitch is really an embroidery stitch, generally used for fine lines and details.

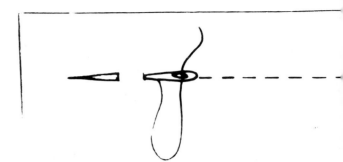

Running Stitch. *To make a running stitch, weave the needle in and out through the fabric layers. The stitches should be small and of an even length. With practice you may take several stitches on the needle at one time.*

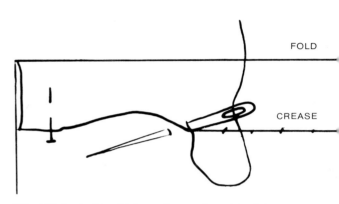

FOLD

CREASE

Slip Stitch. *A slip stitch produces almost invisible stitches. Bring the needle through the fold of the allowance, picking up one or two threads of ground fabric at the same point. Keep the stitches about $\frac{1}{2}''$ apart.*

Backstitch. *Since a backstitch is really an embroidery stitch, generally used for fine lines and details, it's shown here with a double line to represent the thread. Bring the thread through on the stitch line; then take a small backward stitch through just the ground fabric. Bring the needle through again, a little in front of the first stitch; take another backward stitch; and insert the needle at the point where it first came through.*

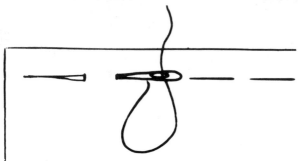

Basting. *Basting is temporary and the stitches are used to hold fabric in place until it's stitched. Space the stitches evenly, about ¼" long and ¼" apart. Do not pull the thread too tightly or stretch fabric.*

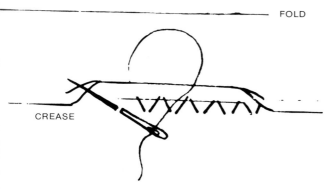

FOLD

CREASE

Blind Stitch. *A blind stitch is almost invisible on both sides. The thread will be hidden in the fold of the allowance. Bring the thread through the fold near the edge, picking up a tiny stitch of ground fabric. Reinsert the needle into the fold, pass the needle inside the fold about ½", and take another stitch into the ground fabric.*

However, when you come to the end of your thread, or when you're finished sewing, taking one or two of these stitches on the back of your work will secure your sewing and eliminate the need for a knot. Bring the thread through on the stitch line; then take a small backward stitch through just the ground fabric. Bring the needle through again a little in front of the first stitch, and take another backward stitch inserting the needle at the point where it first came through.

BASTING

Bastings are temporary stitches. They're most valuable to the beginner, but not always necessary. Space your stitches evenly, about ¼" long and ¼" apart; begin and end these stitches with backstitches instead of knots. This allows the stitches to be pulled out more easily.

BLIND STITCHES

The blind stitch is inconspicuous on both sides of the fabric and can be used where two pieces of fabric are turned in on one another, such as the edge of a quilt. Fold the hems of both pieces of fabric in on one another; using a single knotted thread, take a tiny stitch through the folded edge of the backing fabric and then through the folded edge of the frontpiece, burying your stitches in the folds.

The blind stitch can also be used to make an inconspicuous heading (to slip a hanging rod through) for a banner or to finish the edges of a piece. To make a heading for a banner, first crease under about ½" of fabric at the top of the piece, then fold the fabric back to the desired depth, enough to accommodate a hanging rod. From the inside of the crease bring your needle through the fabric but slightly under the crease, picking up a tiny stitch on the back of the ground fabric. Reinsert the needle into the fold slightly under the crease. Pass your needle inside the fold about ½" and take another tiny stitch into the back. Repeat till hem is complete.

MACHINE APPLIQUÉ

The sewing machine can be a great asset to your work. The decision to appliqué by machine or hand depends on several factors. Machine appliqué is preferable when the finished article is intended for hard use—such as a child's garment or toy—or will be frequently laundered—such as bed linens. For no matter how careful your handwork, under hard wear it generally won't have the holding power of locked, machine stitches.

Time is another factor to consider. There's no doubt that plain machine stitchery goes faster than handwork, and if you're working on a large project, such as a bed throw, the machine will certainly expedite your work. Aside from these practical considerations, most machines today have attachments that embroider decorative stiches such as scallops and zigzag motifs. You may want to incorporate one or more of these bold, wide stitches into your design.

A FORGIVING MEDIUM

There are few hard and fast, "one-way-only" rules in appliqué. Whatever stitches or technique you use to achieve the effect you want is right for you, regardless of whether this is the way someone else does it or not. As problems arise, each of you will work out solutions that seem most natural for you. So gather your fabrics, ideas, tools, and confidence; appliqué is a very "forgiving" medium.

4
EMBROIDERY STITCHES

Embroidery adds a delightful dimension to appliqué and offers all manner of creative possibilities. It serves to embellish, enrich, and emphasize your designs and allows you to make the design more intricate or to add a line-drawing quality where needed.

The basic stitches illustrated in this chapter give you a beginner's vocabulary with which to work. Experiment with these stitches. Use different textures of yarn; try working each stitch in a tight, neat pattern and in a loose, casual one. Work them in rows and circles, flowerlike forms, and abstract shapes. You'll be surprised at the variety of effects possible with each stitch.

Counting variations, there are literally hundreds of embroidery stitches, and later as your skill and interest grow, you'll want to investigate some of the more intricate ones. There are any number of well-illustrated books on embroidery to help you.

USES OF EMBROIDERY

Embroidery is the answer to the need for textural quality and more intricate design in small areas. A visual textural quality, of course, can be achieved with fabric having a printed pattern, but embroidery adds a three-dimensional textural quality that's enriching. The wings of the butterfly (p. 41) could have been appliquéd in printed fabric, but the effect wouldn't be as rich and delicate as embroidery.

Since small, involved shapes are difficult to handle in appliqué, you can break down basic appliqué shapes into additional areas of texture and pattern with embroidery. The medallions on the wing of the owl wall hanging (p. 48) were first appliquéd in a solid color fabric, then embroidered over with a number of different stitches that form textured patterns; this embroidery gives the wanted richness and depth to these small areas. Features on the sun's face in the wall hanging (p. 43) and body details of *Howard the Strong Man* (p. 44) exemplify the use of embroidery to add the quality of a line drawing.

STRAIGHT STITCH

The straight stitch is a single stitch of any length. Unlike the running stitch (Chapter

Cannon *by Diantha Fielding. Running stitches are used to represent smoke. The long, thin stripes of material were fringed on the edges to suggest the force and activity of a blast.*

Embroidery Stitches 35

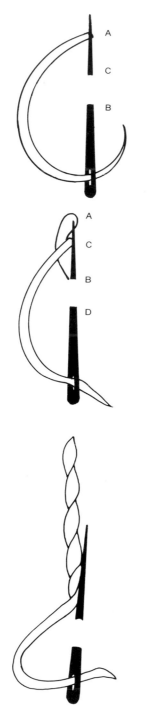

Stem Stitch

Step 1. *To make the stem stitch, bring the thread to the front of the fabric (at A). Insert the needle at B and bring it up again at C.*

Step 2. *For the second stitch, insert the needle at D bringing it out at B.*

Step 3. *The stem stitch produces a continuous line of stitches.*

3), which is a series of evenly spaced straight stitches, the straight stitch may vary in length and may be worked in a regular or irregular manner depending upon the effect you want. The only caution is that the stitch should not be too long, or it will have to be tacked down to remain in place.

STEM STITCH

The stem stitch is used to make a continuous line, such as the features on the sun's face (p. 43), or as its name implies, for plant stems and branches.

Bring the needle through from the back of the fabric at A. Hold the working thread either to the right, or to the left of the needle, but keep the thread consistently on one side. Reinsert the needle at B, out at C, and draw the thread through to complete your first stitch. Insert the needle at D, out at B, and draw the thread through to complete your second stitch.

SATIN STITCH

The satin stitch is used to fill an area solidly. The stitches may be slanted or they may lie straight across the work area, as shown in the shirt front (p. 44).

To begin, lightly outline the shape on your fabric with a soft pencil. Start in the center of the shape and bring the needle through from the back of the fabric at A. To establish an angle (if you want a slant), insert the needle at B and bring it out close to A. Work up to the top; then start again at the center, and work down to the bottom. It is important to maintain a crisp edge with stitches worked evenly next to one another.

CHAIN STITCH

The chain stitch (it looks like a chain) may be used as a border or outline stitch or worked in close rows to fill in an area. The children of Chijnaya, Peru, use the chain stitch almost exclusively in their charming pictorial embroideries. The example pictured (p. 42) shows the chain stitch both filling and outlining areas.

Starting at the top of the line to be covered, bring your needle through from the back of the fabric at A. Insert the needle right next to A; bring it out at B. The

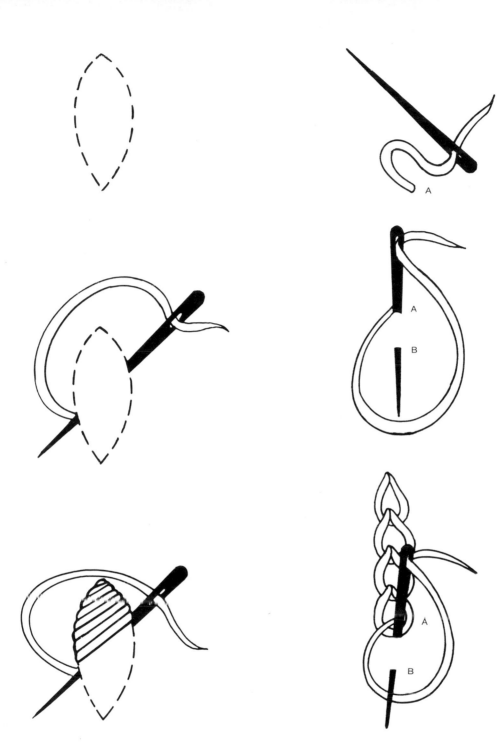

Satin Stitch
Step 1. *Mark the outline of the shape you want to make with the satin stitch.*

Step 2. *Start in the center and keep the same slant to the stitch.*

Step 3. *After finishing one end, again start in the center and finish the other end.*

Chain Stitch
Step 1. *To form a chain stitch, bring the needle through the fabric at A.*

Step 2. *Insert the needle close to A and bring it out at B.*

Step 3. *Draw the thread through the fabric and over the loop of working thread.*

Embroidery Stitches   37

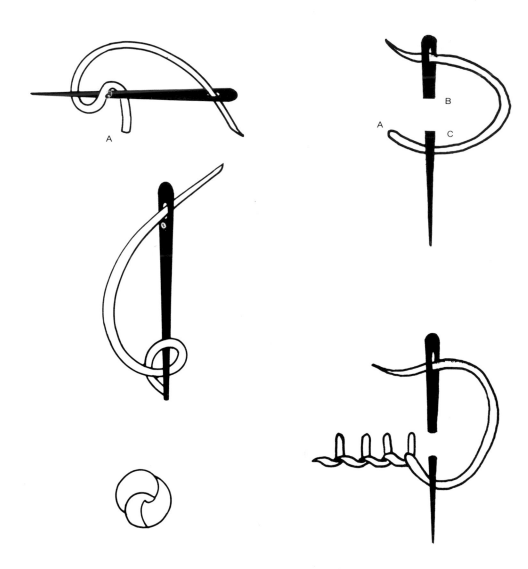

French Knot
Step 1. *Bring the needle through the fabric at A and wrap the working thread around the needle once or twice to make a French knot.*

Step 2. *Insert the needle close to A and pull the twists gently until they are snug.*

Step 3. *The size of the finished French knot depends on the weight of the thread or yarn.*

Buttonhole Stitch
Step 1. *For a buttonhole stitch, bring the needle through the fabric at A. Insert it at B and bring it out at C.*

Step 2. *The working thread is held under the needle.*

distance depends on the length of stitch you want. Draw the thread through fabric and over the loop of working thread.

FRENCH KNOTS

French knots may be scattered at random over an area to give a textural effect. They can be worked in rows, as on the rooted bulb (p. 47) or placed close together to fill an area (p. 46).

Bring your needle through from the back of the fabric at A. Hold the working thread in your left hand and wrap it around the needle once or twice. Insert the needle right next to A; pull the twists gently till they are snug but not tight around the needle. Then draw the needle through to the back of the piece. The size of the knot depends on the weight of the thread or yarn.

BUTTONHOLE STITCH

The buttonhole stitch may be used for appliquéing, giving the shapes a decorative edge, or as a decorative stitch in itself. You can work it in a circle with spikes radiating in or out to form small flowers, or you can use it in straight rows to fill in an area.

Work from left to right. Bring the needle through from the back of the fabric at A. Insert the needle at B, bring it out at C, straight down from B and in line with A.

The working thread is held under the needle as shown, forming a straight line along the bottom.

EMBROIDERED LETTERING

Banners and wall hangings are natural areas for mottos and sayings. It's simpler and far more effective to embroider any small lettering for them than to try to appliqué such tiny, involved shapes. The finished effect is charming when you embroider these in your own handwriting. Write or print your motto on the ground fabric with soft pencil, then embroider over this pencil outline. The stem stitch, chain stitch, or satin stitch may be used for lettering.

APPLIQUED LETTERING

Appliquéd lettering on larger projects should be simple block shapes. The lettering needn't be formally regular in shape or spacing because a certain irregularity adds a sense of spontaneity and charm to your work. (See the personal banner of Esther Feldman on pages 40 and 77.) Experiment with letters cut out of paper first, rearranging the spacing and changing the shapes until you're pleased with the effect. After appliquéing, you can embellish the letters with embroidery over or around for added richness and depth.

Primary Alphabet. *For those occasions when your design calls for printing, here's a primary alphabet for you to refer to.*

Embroidered Printing. *Detail of* A Bird in the Bush, *(p. 88). Small lettering that would be difficult to handle in appliqué may be embroidered. First print the motto on the banner. Then embroider over the letters with stem stitches.*

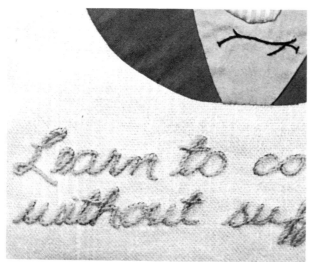

Embroidered Cursive Letters. *The motto of this throw pillow made by Diantha Fielding was embroidered with stem stitches before the pillow was assembled.*

Felt Lettering. *Detail of* Personal Banner, *(p. 77). The designed irregularity of the felt lettering on this banner adds a quality of spontaneity to the piece.*

Butterfly *(Above). Detail of* Personal Banner, *(p. 66). A combination of simple stitches enrich the wings of this fanciful butterfly. Running stitches and stem stitches define the borders of the upper wings. Straight stitches and satin stitches combine for the design in the center of each upper wing. Running stitches form curvilinear designs on the lower wings.*

Leaves *(Left). Detail of* A Bird in the Bush, *(p. 88). The leaves are appliquéd with a simple running stitch. The circular forms are made of satin stitches.*

Child's Landscape. *This is a detail of embroidery work by a child of Chijnaya, Peru. The chain stitch is used exclusively in this piece to both outline and fill areas.*

Eye of the Sun. *Detail of* Sunflower Sun, *(p. 68). The iris of the eye is formed by button-hole stitches which have been worked closely together to make a circle.*

Body Features *(Left). Detail of* Howard the Strong Man, *(p. 88). Stem stitches are used to draw body details on this figure. The bold exclamation mark on the shirt front is made of satin stitches, worked straight across.*

Bouquet *(Above). Detail of* Tattooed Lady, *(p. 87). Stem stitches worked over one another give the desired bunched effect to the flower stems in this bouquet. The flower heads are lazy daisy stitches with a scattering of French knots.*

Anatomy of a Flower *(Left). This is a detail of a cross section of a flower interpreted in appliqué. Chain stitches worked in cotton floss trace the path of pollen down the center of the pistil. French knots represent pollen on the stamen heads.*

Tulip Bulb *(Above). Detail of Tulip Quilt, (p. 77). French knots worked in curving lines increase the textural quality of this tulip bulb. Detached buttonhole stitches form the roots.*

Owl's Wing *(Left). Detail of* Owl Saying Good-by, *(p. 109). A great variety of embroidery stitches, such as the running stitch, French knot, fly stitch, boullion stitch, and Van Dyke stitch, add texture to the appliqué. A good book on embroidery will prove helpful if you like embellishing your appliqué with several types of stitches.*

Owl's Eye *(Above). Detail of* Owl Saying Good-by, *(p. 109). A variety of stitches form the eye. The center is satin stitches surrounded by circles of chain stitches with radiating spokes of stem stitches.*

5
SMALL HOUSEHOLD ITEMS

Small household and gift items are excellent projects for beginners, as well as more advanced stitchers. Toys, bed and table linens, cushion covers, chair seat covers, hotpads, pot holders, and garments are all candidates for appliqué, and depending upon your life style, you can probably think of a dozen others. Everyday articles take on new dimension when personalized with your own ideas. They're more fun to use, and they're visual reminders of your skill and ability, or just plain doggedness in seeing a project through to completion.

And as anyone who has ever received a gift made by the giver can tell you, that gift is cherished for meaning far beyond any utilitarian character it may have. It needn't be elaborate; it can be as small as a hotpad, as simple as a headscarf.

But look out! You can get so gleeful with this medium that you may be tempted to make what Betty MacDonald of *Egg and I* fame called "toe covers"—useless covers for things that need no covers, like cleaner containers, telephones, and wastebaskets. Appliquéing is fun, but it's even more fun when you have a legitimate use for the article you're making. This chapter shows some examples of finished articles and offers some suggestions that you can adapt to your own needs and designs.

PLACEMATS

Placemats are fun to work on because there are so many possibilities. You can make a set with all the mats identical in color and design, or you might want to consider several alternatives. For instance, the ground color of the mats can be the same, with the design repeated in varying prints or colors on each. Or the ground fabric can be of different colors with the design carried out in the same material on each mat. You might choose a favorite theme, perhaps flowers or fruits, and appliqué a different one on each mat. Children especially enjoy mats that are personalized.

The design can either fill the center of the mat or frame the setting. If you like the feel of a more substantial mat, after you've completed the appliqué, back the mat with a bright contrasting color or a gay print. For a final flourish, coordinate napkins

Geometric Placemats *by Diantha Fielding. These were designed to accommodate four place settings. They were made of various cottons and machine appliquéd.*

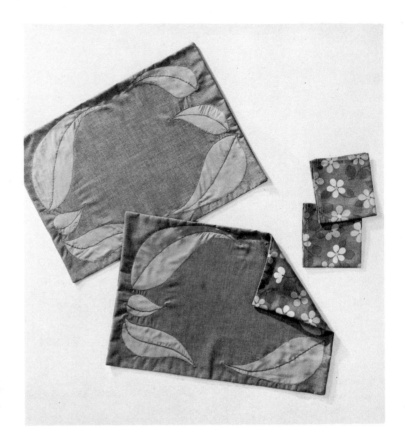

Leaf Design *by Diantha Fielding. Cotton percale appliqué on kettle cloth ground. The use of color needn't be realistic. Here the leaf shapes on the top mat are blue while those on the bottom mat are lavender; both on spring green ground material. The appliqué and the scalloped edging on the napkins were done by machine.*

Flame Design *by Diantha Fielding. The shapes were cut freehand, placed in the center of the placemats and the hotpad, and machine appliquéd. Each design is slightly different although the overall effect is the same. The hotpad was interlined with four layers of lightweight cotton blanket material.*

with your placemats by making the napkins of the same fabric used to back the mats or of the material used for the appliqué motifs. A good size for a dinner napkin is 16″ x 16″. Remember that napkins should be made of soft, absorbent cotton because fabric with too hard a finish, such as denim, will produce the perplexing effect of trying to blot with a piece of oilcloth.

For the ground fabric for your placemats, use washable serviceable-weight material such as denim, duck, or kettle cloth. If the placemats are to be used often and therefore frequently laundered, the sewing machine is the most appropriate way of appliquéing. For a placemat, a generous size, say 14″ x 18″, accommodates a dinner place setting without crowding. For four mats, 1 yard of 45″ wide material is sufficient for the ground fabric and leaves you some good-sized scraps. When you cut, allow $\frac{5}{8}$″ all around the placemat for a hem. If you want to back the mats, first complete your appliqué; then place the right side of the mat and the right side of the backing fabric together. Stitch around three sides of the placemat and about 4″ from each corner of the fourth side. Turn right-side out and close the opening with slip stitches.

SHEETS AND PILLOW CASES

Appliqué on ready-made sheets and pillow cases adds a custom touch to these necessary household items and makes them a joy to use. Sheets and case are available in a wide range of lovely colors so you'll have no difficulty finding those that fit in with your decorating scheme. The linens pictured on page 70 show a design repeated three times along the top sheet turndown and once on each case. Simple stem stitches embellish the design, along with appliquéd lettering on one of the cases.

This is one approach, but there are numerous alternatives. A train or animals running along the border would be charming for a child's room. You can get a coordinated look for the room by repeating the design on window curtains.

Appliqué fabric should be washable cotton, such as percale. If the sheets and pillow cases are the no-iron variety, your appliqué fabric should be also.

HOTPADS AND POT HOLDERS

Hotpads can be square, round, oval, or rectangular. If you wish, you can coordinate your hotpads with your placemats (p.52) and thereby avoid the mismatched "nothing goes together" linen closet syndrome.

The size of the pads is determined by the size of your serving dishes. Depending on the desired shape, use a square or rectangular baking dish or an inverted dinner plate as your pattern. Place the dish on your ground fabric and trace around it lightly. Cut the fabric $\frac{1}{2}$″ larger all around than the desired finished size to allow for hemming. To be functional, the hotpad should have three layers — top, inner layer, and backing. The inner layer may be cotton batting, flannel, or an old piece of toweling. All materials should be washable.

The design can be appliquéd on the ground fabric first, and the three layers assembled by stitching them together around the edge, turning the hems of the top and bottom layer in on one another. Or you can proceed as follows:

Pin the appliqué shapes on the ground fabric; then pin the three layers together around their edges. Using the longest stitch on your sewing machine, first baste around the edges of the appliqué shapes, through all three layers; then go around the edge of the pad. By basting first, you prevent the shapes from puckering when you do the final sewing. Using the satin stitch setting on your zigzag attachment, stitch over your bastings; then trim around the pad's edges.

Pot holders are made in the same manner. They should be large enough and sufficiently padded to serve their purpose.

JACKET LINING

Appliquéing a design on a jacket lining may seem baroque as all get out, but what pleasure it will give you. Even if you don't take the jacket off, you know the handwork is there. It's much easier to do the appliquéing before the lining is inserted in the garment. You can loosen the lining of a ready-made jacket and do the appliqué work, but that's a difficult project.

Garment linings are generally of light-

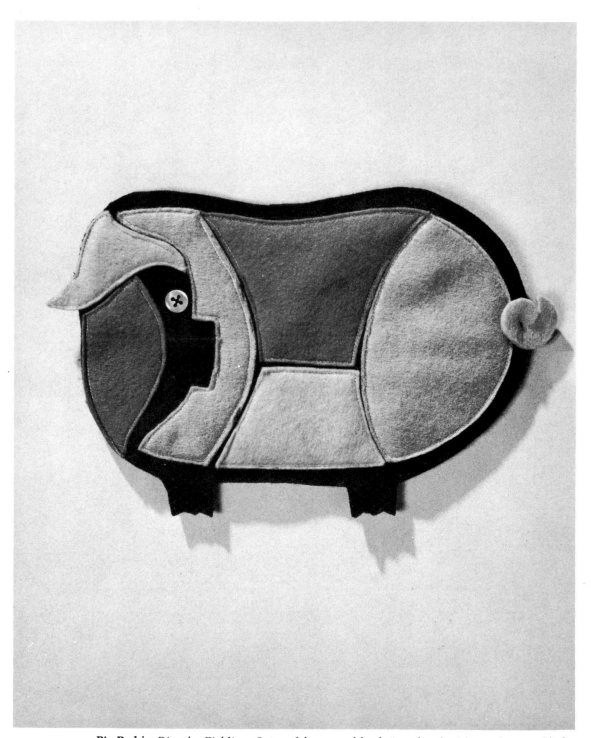

Pig-Pad *by Diantha Fielding. Cotton felt top and back, interlined with two layers of light-weight cotton blanket material. This pot holder was inspired by a diagram of meat cuts. The button eye and quotation mark tail add touches of whimsy.*

Jacket Lining *(Above) by Diantha Fielding. Wool challis appliqué on silk peau de soie lining. The center circle was appliquéd in two parts, one on either side of the pleat.*

Ecology Skirt *(Left) by Evangeline Shears. The design is worked in various colors of cotton percale on navy-blue denim. The appliqué was added before the side seams were stitched.*

Honeybee and Comb *by Diantha Fielding. Cotton percale appliqué on kettle cloth ground. The honeybee and comb design, machine appliquéd in bright colored percale, makes a charming seat cover for this antique bentwood chair. The front and back legs of the bee are outlined in stem stitches.*

weight, silklike quality, and the appliqué pieces should be of similar weight. For the appliquéd design to be effective, the lining should be made of an unprinted fabric. Think in terms of the middle back as the design area. A few basic shapes that can be coordinated into a design work best. Most jacket linings have a center pleat to allow for ease, so keep this in mind when planning your design. If any part of the design is to fall across the pleat, it must be done in two parts in such a manner that it looks like one piece.

Cut your shapes and arrange them on the lining until you're pleased with the effect; then pin them in place. Hand appliqué using the slip stitch because you want a delicate effect.

THROW PILLOWS AND CHAIR SEAT COVERS

Throw pillows and chair seat covers are projects that give you a great deal of satisfaction. The mechanics of making a pillow or covering a chair seat aren't difficult. Whether due to untrained terriers or children in the throes of creative expression, most of us have had to re-cover both pillows and chair seats in our homemaking careers. If you want to make a pillow from scratch, you can buy fillers such as kapok or pillow forms of the desired shape. The appliqué area is small and, therefore, quickly completed. In no time, you have a useful, colorful article that adds lively color interest to your room.

When planning a pillow, consider where and by whom it will be used. If it's for a living room that doesn't get much wear and tear or a feminine boudoir, it can be made of a lush or fragile fabric and appliquéd by hand. A pillow for the den or children's room calls for sturdy, washable fabrics and machine appliqué so you won't panic when you find the children nesting among your handwork eating peanut butter and jelly sandwiches.

Young children enjoy fanciful pillows with secret hiding places for small treasures, such as the one shown above right. This one includes a pajama pocket in the back. To make this, you'll need three rectangles of fabric—two to form the pillow and a third that is machine-hemmed at the top and left open to form a pocket for the pajamas.

Pocket Pillow *by Diantha Fielding. Cotton percale, 14" x 20". Children like secrets and surprises, and this pillow has an abundance of secret openings where small treasures can be hidden. In the back is a large pocket made for pajamas. All the shapes are machine stitched for sturdiness.*

Stuffed Animals *by Sherby Barber. This menagerie of animals—the friendly lion, smug pussycat, and shy skunk—were machine appliquéd, then sewn together, and stuffed with kapok. The simple embroidery embellishments of whiskers, mouths, the cat's eyes, and the skunk's flower were added after the animals were stuffed.*

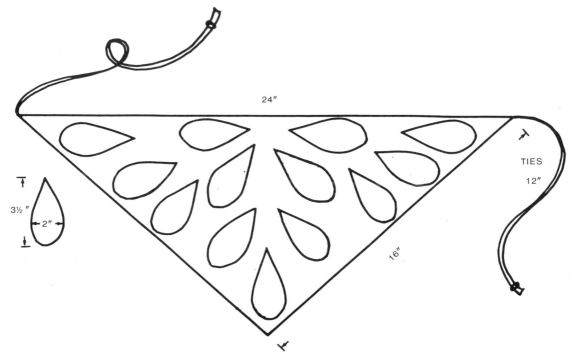

24"

3½ "

2"

TIES

12"

16"

The pattern (Above) for the headscarf, designed by Diantha Fielding, shows the sizes and shapes of the different pieces and where to place them. Below is the finished headscarf.

To remain crisp looking, chair seat covers should be made of washable, durable fabrics and machine appliquéd. To make a chair seat cover, first make a paper pattern in the shape of the seat. Pin the pattern to the backing fabric and cut the fabric 3″ or 4″ larger all around than the pattern to allow for the turnunder and the depth of padding. When your appliqué work is complete, spray the cover with a soil-retarding fabric protector such as Scotchgard.

MAKING A HEADSCARF

This is a simple project that a beginner can enjoy doing. The ground fabric of the scarf can be a plain color with the appliquéd leaves cut from printed fabric or a contrasting color. The lining can be a contrasting plain color or a print.

MATERIALS

1. Three pieces of washable cotton, two slightly larger than 16″ x 24″ and one large enough for the thirteen leaf shapes.

2. Two narrow pieces of fabric for the ties.

3. Scissors.

4. Safety pins.

5. Dressmaker pins.

6. Needle and thread.

CUTTING OUT AND APPLIQUÉING

1. Cut two pieces of the washable cotton into triangles 16″ x 16″ x 24″ for the ground fabric and the lining.

2. Cut out thirteen leaf shapes, each approximately 3½″ x 2″.

3. Cut out two lengths of fabric, each 12″ x 1″, for the ties.

4. Arrange the leaf shapes on the ground fabric and pin them into place.

5. Turn under ¼″ at the edges of each leaf shape, mitering the ends, and appliqué them into place.

MAKING THE TIES

6. Fold the ties in half lengthwise, right sides of the fabric facing, and machine stitch ¼″ from the edge. Trim the seam close to the stitching.

7. Pin a safety pin at one end and push it through the tube of fabric to turn the ties right side out. Press and tie a knot at one end of each tie.

ASSEMBLING THE HEADSCARF

8. Lay the appliquéd triangle right side up and pin the unknotted ends of the ties at either end of the long side of the triangle.

9. Pin the right side of the lining to the right side of the top of the scarf with the ties curled up inside.

10. Machine stitch the two short sides of the triangle and 9″ at either end of the long side, leaving about a 6″ opening at the top.

11. Clip the corners close to the stitching. Turn the scarf right side out and stitch the opening together. Press.

6
QUILTS

Few projects offer so many rewards as making a quilt. The work itself is fascinating and tranquilizing. The finished piece serves a definite physical function, but it's also decorative and has charm and meaning money can't buy. You can work on it alone or get a sewing circle together and, in a spirit of "many hands make light work," help assemble one another's quilts while you visit and chat about whatever women have chatted about since the time of Eve.

DESIGN SOURCES

The key to a successful quilt is to draw on your own life and memory for design. Anything worth putting in the photo album—happy family events, comforting memories—in fact anything you love can be recorded on a quilt. On a king-size quilt one stitcher commemorated a vacation trip she and her husband took to Europe. Appliquéd in bright-colored cottons with touches of embroidery, various blocks show their small car piled high with luggage, a wonderful old nun outside the Vatican, the gondola in Venice, a palace guard in England (looking for all the world like a Gilbert and Sullivan soldier), a windmill in Holland, a stoic country-woman balancing a jug of water on her head, and many other warm and funny stitchery memories.

The quilt shown on the frontis was made by Mrs. DeEtte White for her granddaughter. The central panel features the granddaughter wearing the red shoes she loves. Surrounding panels are appliquéd with fanciful flowers, birds, and butterflies—a child's garden of delight. Some of the designs on this quilt were from a commercial pattern. Others are Mrs. White's.

A number of years ago, Diantha Fielding began making baby quilts for the first-born of her married friends. Her designs were a free interpretation of the traditional Tree of Life motif. The baby's name and birthdate were embroidered on the quilt, and as new babies arrived in these families, their names and birthdates were also documented. Such memory and presentation quilts are a time-honored tradition that goes back to the beginning of our nation.

HISTORY OF QUILT MAKING

The story of quilt making in America is a true rags to riches story. From little more than rags, American women invented the American patchwork or piecework quilt. Every household had its ragbag and into it went every usable scrap of cloth. Cloth was hard to come by in those days and had to be used and reused till the threads disintegrated. Quilting, of course, had been done throughout Europe from the time the Crusaders brought the technique back from the Middle East in the eleventh and twelfth centuries, and the first quilts made here were of the "crazy quilt" variety—a kind of work that had been done in England. Scraps were pieced together in whatever way gave the most mileage, with little thought given to overall design. Gradually around the end of the Revolutionary War, our women began to piece their bits and scraps together in symbolic patterns, and a unique kind of work never seen anywhere before—the American patchwork quilt—was born. Symbolism held an important place in American Indian culture, and it's interesting to speculate on whether or not the idea of symbolic patchwork evolved from exposure to Indian design.

Since it's easier—and there's less waste too—to sew two pieces of cloth together with a straight seam, the designs were geometric, developed from the square, triangle, diamond, and rectangle. The quilts recorded the things the women saw around them in their daily lives, the events of their time, their personal joys and sorrows, and comforting memories of other homes and other times with patterns such as Indian Hatchet, Log Cabin, Flying Geese, Washington's Plume, Delectable Mountains, Bear's Track, Churn Dash, Rocky Road to Kansas, and stars named for every state in the Union. These ingenious women developed a hardship craft into a true art form. It's been said that the history and economic conditions of early America can be traced through quilts. They didn't consider themselves artists, but many examples of their work hang in museums and collections for us to admire. Their craftsmanship was superb; their designs were beautiful and moving.

Putting one piece of cloth on top of another to form a design was a costly luxury so the appliquéd quilt generally wasn't seen here until the end of the seventeenth century, a relatively prosperous time when cloth was more readily available. The symbolic, geometric designs of patchwork gave way to the curves and arabesques possible with appliqué . Designs became more naturalistic with motifs that included all manner of flowers, trees, birds, animals, and human figures too.

We don't make a quilt out of necessity today, for an abundance of beautiful ready-mades are available at reasonable prices. We make them because we want something uniquely our own, because we want to record our own time and the things we love in our own way. As long as this creative urge remains, our quilts will be as personally expressive, our designs as honest and full of vitality as were our grandmother's.

BASIC QUILTING MATERIALS

To make a quilt, you'll need a top which has the appliquéd design, an interlining, and a backing. The top can be made with an overall appliqué design on a ground of the desired size or can be made by appliquéing individual blocks of regular or irregular size that are then sewn together to form the top. The interlining can be Dacron batting (preferable to cotton batting because it doesn't wad up when washed) or a blanket made of one of the synthetic materials. Batting gives a puffier effect than the blanket. The fabric for top and back can be cotton or lightweight wool. Colored or printed sheets of the desired size make an effective back. If you want your quilt to be washable, make sure all the materials used are colorfast and preshrunk.

Quilting is the technique of joining the three layers of your quilt together. You'll need special needles called "betweens"; they're short and sharply pointed. You'll also need quilting thread that is strong and has a smooth finish to allow the thread to glide easily through the layers of material.

If a full-sized quilt seems like an overwhelming project, consider making a carriage or crib-sized one first. You'll find the smaller size more comfortable to handle. When you've had this experience, you can confidently plan a large quilt.

Quilting by Outlining. *Detail of* Mulberry Bush Quilt, *(p. 84). One of the simplest ways to quilt is to outline the appliquéd shapes with running stitches. Outlining emphasizes the design while holding the three layers of the quilt in place. However, if the appliquéd shapes are spaced far apart, additional lines of quilting are needed to keep all of the layers firmly in place.*

Quilting with Diagonal Lines. *Quilt by Mrs. Mary Rawlings. These diagonal lines of quilting are done with thread the same color as the ground fabric. They create a simple, patterned background for the bright orange and yellow flowers and deep-green stems and leaves. A bolder quilting effect would detract from this appliquéd design.*

BASIC QUILTING PROCEDURE

The traditional quilting stitch is a simple running stitch. These stitches are usually very small, evenly spaced, and close together. With experience and depending on the thickness of your fabrics, it's possible to take several stitches at a time on your needle. But at first, to assure the uniformity of your stitches, take them one at a time using two separate movements.

To begin, make a knot at the end of a single strand of thread and bring the needle through from the back to the top of the quilt. Tug gently on the thread till the knot pulls through the back and is buried in the interlining. Now for your two-step quilting stitch. Hold your left hand under the quilt. With your right hand, push the needle straight down (not at an angle); receive it with your left hand and draw the thread through. With your left hand, push the needle straight up, receive it with your right and draw the thread through. When your quilting is completed, take one or two backstitches to secure your sewing, and run the end of the thread into the interlining.

The light and shadow effect of quilting throws your appliqué work in relief. Background quilting can be done in straight rows, crisscross lines, half circles that form cloud or wave patterns, or whatever patterns you feel will most enhance your work. One of the easiest and most effective means of quilting an appliquéd design is simply sewing around the motifs, repeating their shape. The only caution here is to make sure your quilting is sufficient to hold the three layers of material in place. In other words, if your appliqué motifs are spaced far apart you'll have to sew a number of rows of quilting around them so that the interlining doesn't take on a life of its own and begin to wander.

THE QUILTING FRAME

A quilting frame is a wooden device that holds the three layers of material secure and taut while you're quilting. It can be a quilting hoop that looks like an enormous embroidery hoop; it allows you to work on a section at a time. It can also be a rectangular frame the size of the quilt or a convenient working portion of the quilt.

Quilting with a Pattern. Whale Quilt *by Diantha Fielding. The quilting lines can become a significant part of the overall design of the quilt. On this crib quilt they depict waves.*

These may be purchased from department stores or needlework shops.

You can make a simple frame from four 1″ x 2″ wooden strips. The length of the wood strips depends on the size of your quilt, but the two longer strips should be 6″ longer than the width of the quilt. The two shorter strips hold these longer ones in place. Fasten the overlapped corners with "C" clamps. Cover the two long bars with muslin and use thumbtacks to hold the muslin in place. You'll baste your quilt back to this when it's ready for the frame. The frame can be supported on chair backs.

ASSEMBLING THE QUILT

To assemble your quilt, first lay the backing out smoothly on the floor. Spread the interlining over the backing, and then place your quilt top over the interlining. Starting from the center, baste the three layers together in a grid or with lines radiating from the center to the edges, making sure there's no excess pulling or bunching.

After your basting is completed, lay one of the long, muslin-covered strips of the frame along the top of the quilt and the other along the bottom. Sew the top and bottom edges of the quilt backing to the muslin securely enough so that it will hold when stretched taut in the frame. Roll the quilt up snugly on the wood strip at one end, leaving 2′ or 3′ free (depending on the length of the side strips of your frame) at the other end to stretch across your frame. Lap the ends of the wood strip at the free end over the two shorter side strips and fasten together with "C" clamps. Adjust the rolled end so that the quilt is taut in the frame and fasten the two remaining corners together. When this section has been quilted, unfasten the clamps and roll the quilt forward on the wooden strips to reveal the next section to be quilted.

WORKING WITHOUT A QUILTING FRAME

While a quilting frame is a great help, it isn't an absolute necessity — particularly if you're working on a small quilt. Even a large quilt can be quilted without a frame, as were a number shown in this chapter.

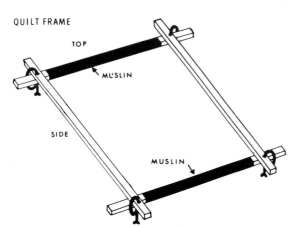

You can make a simple quilting frame from four 1″ x 2″ wooden strips, muslin, thumbtacks, and four C clamps.

Abstract Quilt *by Helen Bitar. Cotton with red ball fringe. Photo by Jacqueline Enthoven. Each brightly colored square was first appliquéd with various shapes. Then they were sewn together. The quilting was done in straight lines along the seams made when the blocks were joined.*

The Juggler of Our Lady *(Above) by Diantha Fielding. Cotton percale, 18" x 30". This was inspired by a French folktale. The panels behind the juggler represent stained-glass windows. The five balls are covered button forms. The covering was first embroidered, then attached to the forms.*

Personal Banner *(Right) by Diantha Fielding. Cotton percale. The hand with a coin in the palm indicates that she is a professional artisan; the butterfly is a symbol of good fortune and domestic bliss. The hand-sewn banner was backed to give it additional weight and a finished appearance.*

Birdcage *(Far Right) by Diantha Fielding. Cotton percale on linen stretched over tempered Masonite, 32" x 56". Embroidery stitches form the decorative wrought iron and the details on the birds.*

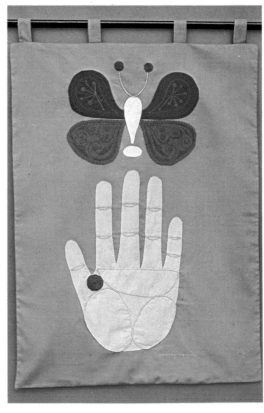

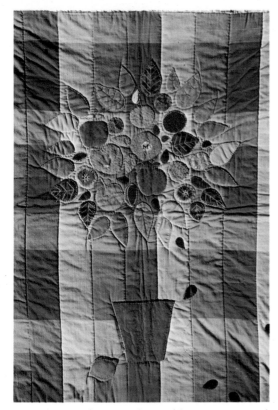

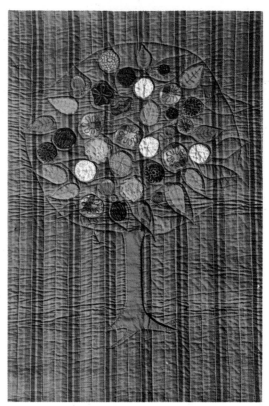

Topiary Tree *by Diantha Fielding. Cotton crib quilt, 45" x 54". This design is based on the Tree of Life motif. The baby's name and birthdate are embroidered on the quilt.*

Jeff's Tree *by Diantha Fielding. Cotton crib quilt, 45" x 54". This is also an interpretation of the Tree of Life theme.*

Sunflower Sun *(Above Left) by Diantha Fielding. Cotton percale on linen stretched over tempered Masonite, 34" x 34". The facial features are drawn with buttonhole stitches and stem stitches in wool yarn. The sun rays are formed with running stitches done in cotton floss.*

San Blas Reverse Appliqué *(Below Left). Photo courtesy of Jacqueline Enthoven. The Indians of the Cuña region in Panama's San Blas Islands make elaborate panels of reverse appliqué. They use the pieces as front and back panels of their yoked, short-sleeve blouses which are called molas. The panels also make attractive wall hangings and covers for cushions.*

Bed Linens *(Above) by Diantha Fielding. It's easy to personalize linens with your own ideas and simple appliqué shapes.*

Silver Dollar Eucalyptus Branch *(Right) by Diantha Fielding. Silk organdy and cotton organza on a background of lightweight, dress-lining material, 96" x 54". An illustration from a seed catalog suggested this design. The light coming through the glass door gives the piece a three-dimensional effect. The piece is hung from a wooden rod slipped through a top hem; another rod at the bottom helps the piece hang properly.*

Praise Banner *by Diantha Fielding. 45" x 62". This Christmas decoration bears an old German proverb. Instead of being sewn, it was appliquéd with white glue.*

Christmas Angel. *Detail of Praise Banner. Only the buttons required needle and thread. The other shapes were attached with glue. The hands were made by covering a cardboard shape with fabric.*

Plucked Dandelion *(Right) by Diantha Fielding. Cotton percale, 32" x 56". The frayed petal ends add texture. Details are embroidered using stem stitches, satin stitches, and French knots. The piece was stretched over tempered Masonite.*

Rose Window *by Diantha Fielding. Cotton-Dacron blend percale, 36" x 36". This piece of reverse appliqué was designed to be hung so that the light filtering through the various layers of fabric will give the piece the quality of stained glass. Detail shown at right.*

Personal Banner *by Esther Feldman, 54" x 45". Miss Feldman chose a heavy, canvaslike material for the ground fabric to give the banner the desired weight.*

Tulip Quilt *by Diantha Fielding. Cotton-Dacron blend percale appliqué on lightweight wool, 90" x 62". The bulb is accented with French knots and the roots are formed with detached buttonhole stitches.*

San Blas Reverse Appliqué *(Left). Photos by Jacqueline Enthoven. Women of the Cuña Indian tribe of the San Blas Islands, Panama, create these designs from scraps of brightly colored cloth. The Cuñas are primitive and have no formal written language. Their designs are very free interpretations of nature (birds, animals, plants), people, their religion, biblical stories—any subject that captures their fancy.*

Short-Sleeve Blouses *(Above and Right). Photos by Jacqueline Enthoven. Indians of the Cuña region in Panama's San Blas Islands make reverse appliqué panels which form the front and back panels of their blouses, called molas.*

Wild Strawberry *(Far Right) by Diantha Fielding. Cotton percale mounted on Masonite before framing, 54" x 36". Photo by George Szanik. This design was based on a cross-section illustration of a flower. The butterflies and the flower details are embroidered.*

WILD STRAWBERRY

Quail *by Tina Orth. Cotton appliqué. Photo by Jacqueline Enthoven. Miss Orth made this when she was a high school student in Seattle. The idea came from the wild quail who live around her home. Embroidery emphasizes and enriches the design.*

If you work without a frame, the important points to keep in mind are that you must have a large enough area to lay your quilt out flat while basting its layers together; your basting stitches should be fairly small; and the rows of basting should be no more than 8" or 10" apart.

FINISHING THE QUILT

When your quilting is completed, trim the edges cutting back any interlining that extends beyond the quilt top and backing. Finish the quilt's edges with blind hemming, bias tape, or matching fabric cut in bias strips about 1" wide and joined together to the proper length.

COVERLETS

Coverlets are made in the same manner as quilts but without an interlining or with a lightweight interlining, such as muslin. If you want to make a coverlet without interlining or quilting, attach the backing to the coverlet top in the following manner. First, press open all seams on the coverlet top. Then, with the right sides of the backing and top facing, machine stitch with ½" seams, leaving an opening for turning. Turn, and use a blind stitch to close the opening. Tack the top and backing together in a number of places to hold them in place.

MULBERRY BUSH QUILT

The following directions for making the Mulberry Bush Crib Quilt serve as a general guide for making your own version of a baby quilt. The finished size is 36" x 45".

There are six pattern pieces in this design: 3 leaf shapes, cut freehand so the sizes vary somewhat on the finished quilt; a 2" circle for the mulberries; a tree trunk; and the bird.

MATERIALS

1. Large sheets of brown wrapping or butcher paper.

2. A flow tip or other type of marking pen.

3. Fabric for top and back. These should be preshrunk, colorfast cottons or cotton-Dacron blends with a soft finish and close weave.

Quilt top: 1¼ yards of solid color fabric 36" wide.

Quilt back: 1¼ yards bright plaid or gingham 36" wide.

4. Appliqué motifs — assorted colors and prints.

5. Interlining — Dacron quilt batting.

6. Edging (optional): 5 yards of cotton piping. 5 yards of 1½" cotton eyelet ruffle. You may dye these to match the background color of the quilt top if you wish.

7. A quilting needle or size 5 or 6 needle for quilting plus regular sewing needles for basting, appliqué work, and finishing edges.

8. Quilting thread or mercerized cotton embroidery thread size 5 or 8 for quilting. Mercerized cotton sewing thread size 50 or 60 for basting and appliqué. Three strands of 6 strand cotton embroidery floss in a dark color to embroider bird's eye and legs.

9. Scissors, pins, and thimble.

CUTTING THE APPLIQUÉ SHAPES

1. Draw the design full scale on the wrapping paper with a marking pen. If the paper isn't large enough, tape two sheets together. Trace the individual motifs onto another sheet of paper to serve as patterns for cutting the fabric. You can tack the full-scale drawing to a door and refer to it as a placement guide.

2. Select the fabric for the quilt top and back and all appliqué pieces before you cut any of the shapes. Pin the patterns on the chosen fabric and cut out the pieces, adding ¼" all around for the turnunder allowance.

MAKING THE PADDED
MULBERRY SHAPES

3. There are twenty-one of these shapes so cut out twenty-one circles. Baste a line of small running stitches around the entire edge of each circle. (The fabric circles are 2" in diameter; the completed mulberries are about 1".)

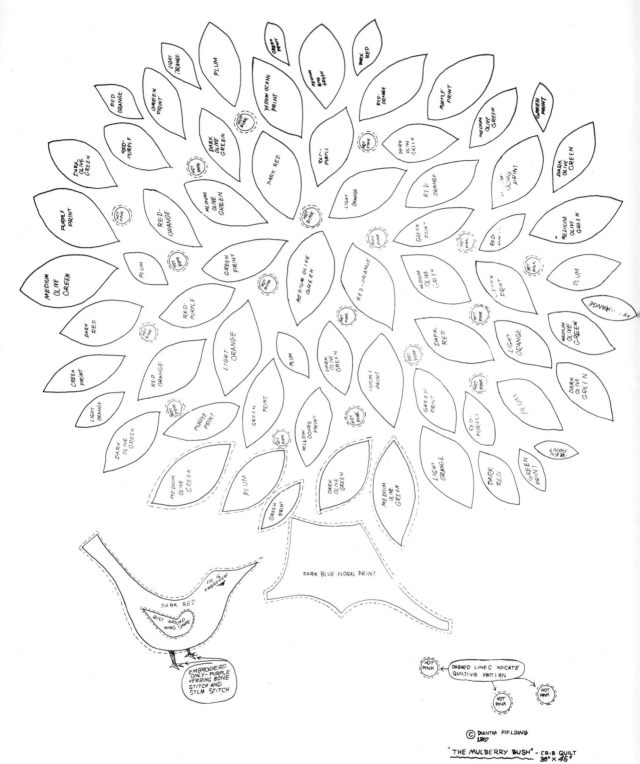

This pattern for the Mulberry Bush Quilt *shows the appliqué shapes with suggestions for their colors and the quilting lines.*

After you have assembled the three layers of material of the quilt, baste them together in a grid pattern.

Mulberry Bush Quilt, *36" x 45". This crib quilt was designed by Diantha Fielding.*

4. Place a wad of Dacron in the center of each circle and pull the basting thread to gather the circle around the Dacron. It will form a little ball. Stitch the edges together and trim off any excess fabric. When you sew the mulberries in place, make sure you attach them to a broad enough base with very secure stitches so that they can't be pulled off.

APPLIQUÉING AND EMBROIDERING THE SHAPES

5. Turn and baste under the ¼" allowance on each of the other pieces. Clip the edges of the allowance where it's necessary on the curves so that the appliquéd piece lies flat. As you baste, miter the end of each leaf to a crisp point. (See Chapter 3 for directions on how to make sharp corners.) These bastings will be removed after each shape is sewn in place.

6. When all of the appliqué pieces are ready, pin them into position on the quilt top. Sew each motif in place using thread of a matching color. Embroider the bird's eye and its legs.

ASSEMBLING AND BASTING THE LAYERS OF THE QUILT

7. When the appliqué work is completed, assemble the three layers of the quilt. Place the quilt back on the floor, wrong side up. Place the batting over the back,

and smooth it out. Place the quilt top over the batting, right side up.

8. Baste the three layers together in a grid pattern. Starting in the center, baste horizontally first, then vertically, then around the four sides about 2" from the edge. Make sure that there's no excess pulling or bunching. It's important to start basting in the center; it prevents the various layers from slipping.

QUILTING AND FINAL DETAILS

9. Now quilt by sewing through the three layers. This design was very simply quilted ¼" from the edge of the motifs. It's not necessary to mark the quilting pattern on such a design; you'll use the shape of the appliquéd pieces as your quilting guide. Use close, running stitches, and make sure that each stitch goes through all three layers. Quilting is usually done in the same color as the fabric to be quilted, but here the thread is an integral part of the design and is a bright-colored cotton thread in sharp contrast to the quilt's top fabric.

10. After your quilting is completed, trim any batting that extends beyond the quilt top and back. Turn the edges of the top and back in on one another and pin them together. Then, slip stitch the top and back together. If you're going to use a piping or eyelet edging, insert the edging into the seam before sewing the edges together.

7
FLAGS
AND
BANNERS

Flags and banners are gay and versatile vehicles for your ideas in appliqué, and they are a perfect medium for capturing popular imagery. Colorful banners brighten shopping malls, public libraries, and department stores all across the country. Museums and galleries also show banners made by serious contemporary artists that reflect the artistic tastes of our time—everything from pop to representational. In the home, banners can make a bold, decorative statement on your walls, or you can fly a flag outside to signal whatever: that you're in residence at your vacation cabin or that the local small fry are welcome to swim in your pool.

HISTORY OF FLAGS AND BANNERS

Men have been rallying around flags for centuries, and while no one knows just who made the first one, it's a good bet it was a symbol of identification for a person or clan. The fierce Vikings were recognized everywhere they went by their fluttering raven banner, a religious symbol to those seafaring warriors. Ancient Egyptian, Greek, and Roman armies marched under their distinctive standards; the Bible refers to the standards of the different Israelite tribes in their desert camp.

Traditionally, the symbolic devices on a flag (flown at right angles from a staff) or banner (suspended from above) represent the principles of a person or group. In other words, they're a quick visual code expressing an idea in a graphic way. Many of the early flags were of religious origin. Venetian mariners flew the winged lion of St. Mark; the red cross of St. George stood for England; and the X-shaped cross on a blue field for St. Andrew and Scotland. The union of the cross of St. George with the cross of St. Andrew marks the union of England and Scotland into the kingdom of Great Britain. Later the cross of St. Patrick, the patron saint of Ireland, was added creating the union flag of Great Britain which the colonists brought to America.

Superb banners, bearing intricate heraldic designs, were very much a part of the pomp and ceremony-loving Middle Ages when heraldry played such an important social role. Leading artists of the age created armorial bearings, and the family

The Tattooed Lady *by Diantha Fielding. Washable cotton-Dacron blend, backed, 36" x 24". Details on the figure were embroidered with running stitches, satin stitches, and stem stitches. This is part of a series of banners based on the sideshow.*

A Bird in the Bush *(Above) by Diantha Fielding. Hung on wood dowel with wood finial on one end, 16" x 24". A whimsical motto inspired this banner. The appliqué shapes are very simple; the key is their meticulous composition. Embroidery supplies the details of the birds and bush, the circular berries, and the lettering.*

Howard the Strong Man *(Right) by Diantha Fielding. Washable cotton-Dacron blend, 36" x 24". Again embroidery is used for the details. The wood dowel is slipped through an open heading.*

symbols and other devices of distinction were symbolic of all that was considered noble and chivalrous during that golden age of knighthood. Beautiful banners were displayed at religious and secular ceremonies, festivals, and pageants. Men went into battle under their personal banners or with their leaders' devices painted on their armor or stitched on their surcoat as a means of identification. In the confusion of battle in those days of unmechanized warfare, it was practically impossible to know who was clobbering whom, or for that matter whom to clobber, unless a man could quickly identify friend or foe.

CHOOSING A DESIGN

The design on a banner can be anything that interests you—animal, vegetable, mineral, or a purely abstract design—as long as it can be drawn. Your banner can include a motto if you wish—a pithy statement of your goals, guiding principles, or an admonition that may be serious or whimsical. A favorite motto or proverb may even suggest the design; this happened with *The Bird in the Bush* banner.

The Juggler of Our Lady banner (p. 66) was suggested by the French folktale of that name. The story tells of a poor juggler who had no gift, other than his talent, to bring to the Virgin Mary. But she was pleased with his unique gift and smiled.

DESIGNING A PERSONAL STATEMENT

Creating a personal house flag or banner with a design that symbolizes your own special areas of interest or those of your family is an intriguing project. An idea for the design might come from your last name: Archer, Wren, Wolf, etc.—all immediately suggest possibilities. There are symbols for almost every profession and craft, and these might be a starting point; or your feeling about your work or your world may inspire a design.

Designer Esther Feldman's delightfully exuberant personal banner (p. 77) is a statement of some of the things in her world that she loves best. To provide weight, Miss Feldman chose a rather heavy, canvaslike material for the background. It worked, but only the most experienced and patient stitchers should use such heavy material because it's difficult to get a needle through the fabric.

The design of Diantha Fielding's personal banner (p. 66) reflects her interest in stitchery. The hand symbolizes that she is an artisan, and the butterfly is a symbol of good fortune and domestic bliss. Made of cotton, the banner was hand sewn and backed to give it added weight and a finished appearance. Embroidery embellishment consists of four simple stitches; the satin stitch, running stitch, backstitch, and straight stitch.

SEASONAL THEMES

Banners with seasonal themes can be rolled up for storage and taken out yearly to become part of your family's holiday traditions. Designed as a Christmas decoration, the *Praise Banner* (p. 72) bears an old German proverb inviting everyone to join the celebration. The 45" x 62" banner is as gay and massive in size as the event it symbolizes. Seasonal banners that are used infrequently and party banners done for dash and effect to be used only once can be appliquéd with a white glue, such as Wilhold, rather than sewn. Of course, any flag intended to fly outside should be securely machine stitched so that it doesn't flap into shreds with the first breeze.

BACKING A BANNER WITH FABRIC

Unless your ground fabric is quite heavy it's best to back your banner with fabric; the added weight helps it hang properly. When you've finished the appliqué work, put the right side of the banner and the right side of the backing fabric together and stitch around three sides. Turn the banner right side out and finish the fourth side. Fabric tabs, to slip a hanging rod through, can be basted in place and sewn when you stitch the banner and backing together. Or make an open heading for the rod by folding the top of the banner under and stitching it down.

TASSELS

For a decorative finish, tassels can be attached to the corners or along the top or bottom of a banner. Many types of tassels are possible so feel free to use all

To make a felt tassel, clip part of the way through the felt to create a fringe. Then starting from one end, roll up the felt and stitch the tassel closed.

You can make tassels of felt (right), of yarn (left), or by combining yarn and felt (center). Beads add further decorative interest.

More Tassels. *Detail of* Personal Banner, *(p. 77). There are any number of combinations you can use to make tassels. Contrasting colors in yarn or felt, small beads, large beads, different types of yarn—all can add their own special touch.*

types and colors of felt, yarn, beads, and other oddments.

MAKING FELT TASSELS

1. Select a piece of felt as wide as you want the tassel long and long enough to provide the desired thickness.

2. Clip into the felt no deeper than three quarters of the way through.

3. Start from one end and roll up the felt. Stitch the end closed.

MAKING YARN TASSELS

1. Cut a piece of cardboard the length you want the tassel to be.

2. Wrap the yarn around the cardboard to the desired thickness.

3. Slip a long piece of yarn under the loops at the top and tie the single piece of yarn into a knot. The tassel will be attached to the banner by the loose ends of this piece of yarn so make sure that they're long enough.

4. Cut the loops at the bottom of the cardboard.

5. Wind a piece of yarn around the tassel about 1″ from the top. Tie it into a knot and clip the ends. Trim the tassel ends evenly.

THE PRAISE BANNER

For a paste-up banner (one that has shapes glued rather than sewn on), choose any material that's heavy enough to prevent the glue from penetrating and staining the surface. Heavy duck, drill, denim, or any sturdy cotton is suitable. Felt is particularly good for applied pieces because it's edges cut clean and won't ravel. Remember to handle cut pieces tenderly so that their edges don't stretch. Any white glue that's transparent when dry may be used as an adhesive.

Keep in mind that pasting isn't as permanent a technique as sewing, and that the piece will obviously suffer from washing or cleaning. However, it's a quick method, and it allows you to use materials you might not consider if you wanted your banner to be washable. If you spray the

Carefully plan the placement of the design for the Praise Banner *on the ground fabric. Remember to allow space for the scallops at the top.*

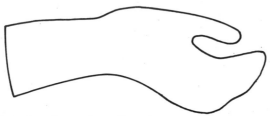

Cut the shape of the hand out of cardboard.

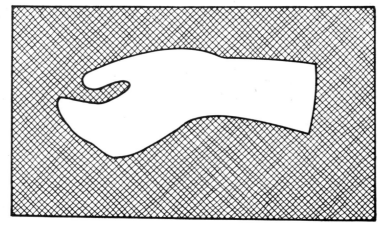

Place the cardboard shape face down on the fabric. Cut out the shape leaving ¼" allowance all around.

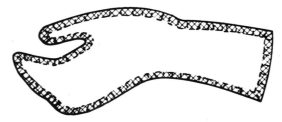

Fold the fabric over the back of the cardboard, clip the curves, and glue it in place.

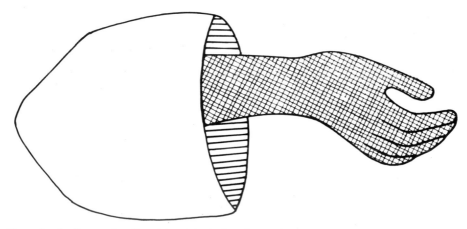

Draw in the finger details with a black, fine-line ink marker or pen.

finished banner with a soil retardant such as Scotchgard, it will remain fresh and crisp-looking for some time. After all, the glued collages that artists such as Picasso and Braque created in the early part of the twentieth century are still around for us to enjoy. (The 45″ x 62″ *Praise Banner* is shown on p. 72.)

MATERIALS

1. White glue.

2. Scissors: an Exacto knife is helpful for cutting small strips of felt.

3. Needle, thread, and pins.

4. Eight pearl buttons.

5. A fine line, permanent-black marking pen.

6. A scrap of lightweight cardboard.

7. 2 yards of 45″ wide Kettle cloth (a textured cotton-Dacron blend) for the ground fabric.

8. ¼ yard each of olive green, avocado green, and white felt.

9. ½ yard each of black and royal blue felt.

MAKING THE BASIC DESIGN

1. Cut the Kettle cloth to the desired size of the background.

2. Experiment with your design on butcher paper until its proportions and lettering are correct; then trace a master pattern with a felt pen.

3. Cut out your pattern; pin the pattern pieces to the felt and cut. Cut the angel's black wings ¼″ larger all around than the white wings.

4. Glue the white wing sections to the larger black wing pieces so that an edge of black shows all around.

5. Pin all the felt pieces on your banner. When you're satisfied with the arrangement, apply the glue to them.

MAKING THE HANDS

6. Cut the shapes of the angel's hands out of lightweight cardboard.

7. Place the cardboard shapes face down on the leftover background fabric. Cut out the shape leaving ¼″ allowance all around.

8. Clip the curves, trim away the excess fabric, and fold the fabric over to the back of the cardboard and glue it in place.

9. Draw in the finger details with a black, fine-line ink marker or pen. Glue the finished hand in place on the ground fabric.

ADDING DETAILS

10. Draw the outline of the head, the facial features and the neck with the felt pen. Glue thin strips of felt along these lines.

11. Sew on the buttons.

MAKING THE SCALLOPS AT THE TOP

12. Fold the fabric over the front, right side to right side, and pin.

13. Using a saucer as a guide, draw an outline of the scallop shapes.

14. Machine stitch along these lines.

15. Cut out the scallops, clip the curves, and turn the fabric right side out.

16. Blind stitch 3″ strips of bias tape to the back of the scallop points to make the loops for the rod. Slip the hanging rod through the loops, and hem the bottom of the banner.

8
WALL HANGINGS

Wall hangings are popular projects with needleworkers. There is understandable pride involved in hanging a piece of your own work to enhance the beauty of your home. Clean line contemporary rooms benefit by the softening contrast of handwork and a wall hanging in a traditional room can add a needed contemporary note. They add warmth and a sense of individuality to any room.

THE DIFFERENCE BETWEEN A BANNER AND A WALL HANGING

The terms banner and wall hanging are sometimes used interchangeably today. However, there still seems to be definite differences between them. A wall hanging *may be* framed or stretched over masonite or plywood, but a banner *never* is. To professional artists who use fabric as a medium, the term wall hanging implies a permanent work of art intended to be hung on an interior wall to be enjoyed in the manner of a painting. A banner *may be* a serious piece of work, but it can also be a quickly made, purely decorative thing to jazz up a garden party or add eye appeal to a football game or political rally or a shopping mall.

MATERIALS

Since mood and subject rather than practicality are important, you can incorporate in a wall hanging whatever found objects or oddments please you and seem to further your design purposes. For instance, artist Lucile Brokaw, whose work has a strong ethnic feeling, has used such non-needlework objects as plastic tails of badminton birdies (p. 104) and thin sheet brass (p. 108) where they helped achieve the feeling she was after in a piece.

Many artists who use fabric as a medium break some of the general rules of appliqué when it serves their aesthetic purpose. Heavy, difficult-to-work-with materials are used in some pieces shown in this chapter. In others the fabric is deliberately frayed to achieve a desired effect.

FINISHING THE SIDES

All sides of a hanging are usually finished in some manner, either by a decorative

Lady *by Gonzalo Duran. Various cottons, linens, and upholstery fabric, 40" x 70". Photo courtesy Zachary Waller Gallery, Los Angeles. The appliqué pieces were machine stitched.*

Mounting a Wall Hanging on Masonite

WHITE GLUE

BOARD

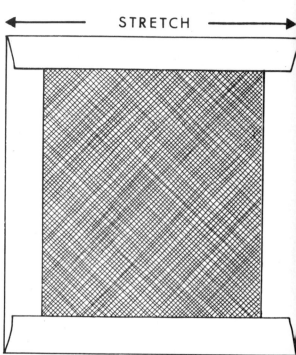

STRETCH

Step 1. *Place the Masonite on the wrong side of the wall hanging. Coat the top edge of the Masonite with white glue.*

Step 2. *Stretch and smooth the fabric across the board.*

MITER CORNERS

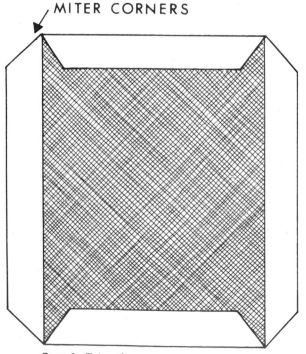

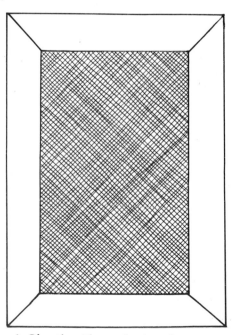

Step 3. *Trim the corners.*

Step 4. *Glue the sides and miter the corners.*

edge, hemming, or backing the piece. Unless the fabric is very heavy, backing is generally preferred so that the piece hangs properly—without rippling or curling at the bottom. When you've finished the appliqué work, put the right side of the hanging and the right side of the backing together and machine stitch around three sides. Turn the hanging right-side out and finish the fourth side. If backing isn't suitable, you can slip a dowel or wood strip into the bottom hem so that it will hang straight.

FINISHING THE TOP

The tops of wall hangings can be finished in several ways. Fabric tabs, through which you slip the hanging rod, can be stitched at spaced intervals along the top. You can also make an open heading for the rod by turning the top of the hanging back sufficiently to accommodate the rod and then stitching it down. Both brass and wood finials are available at hardware stores to give the ends of the rods a decorative finish if you wish. Very large or heavy pieces may require more support and the top of these can be wrapped and tacked around wood two-by-two's.

MOUNTING A WALL HANGING ON MASONITE

You can have your hanging framed by a professional framer, just as you would a painting, but if you're going to frame your work yourself, first stretch it over a piece of Masonite. This will give it a crisp, professional look, and it will also prevent it from sagging.

MATERIALS

1. A piece of ¼″ tempered Masonite, about 2″ smaller than the size of the piece you want to mount.

2. White glue, such as Wilhold.

3. Scissors.

4. Iron.

GLUING THE TOP

1. Press piece.

2. Place piece face down, wrong side up.

3. Place board in the center of the fabric with a 1½″ to 2″ margin all around.

4. Coat the top edge of the board with white glue.

STRETCHING THE FABRIC

5. Turn the top edge of the piece back over the glued area. Smooth the piece out. Working from the center to the sides, stretch the fabric taut from side to side. Keep the edge of the board aligned with a single thread of the fabric running across the top.

6. Allow the glued top to dry.

7. Repeat this process at the bottom of piece and pull the piece very tight. The board will bow slightly, allowing you to stretch the work very, very taut.

TRIMMING THE CORNERS

8. Trim the corners. Cut the excess fabric to a mitered angle.

GLUING THE CORNERS

9. Glue first one side and then the other. Again keep one thread as a guide along the edge of the board.

10. Trim and miter corners and allow the piece to dry.

MOUNTING THE PIECE ON PINE STRETCHER BARS

You can also mount a piece by stretching it over a frame of pine stretcher bars and stapling or tacking it to the back. Stretcher bars, used by artists to stretch canvas for paintings, are available in art supply stores.

To protect and clean a finished piece, spray it with a soil retardant such as Scotchgard and brush it occasionally with a soft, clean brush.

Warrior Ant: Step 1. *To California artist Ted Ball, appliqué is an art form. His creative use of fabric has won wide recognition. After thoroughly researching his subject, he first works out the design on paper.*

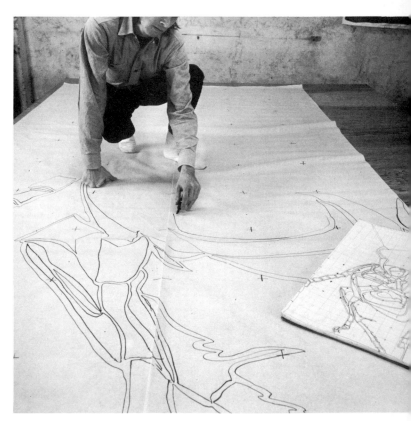

Warrior Ant: Step 2. *With an ink marker, he transfers the design full scale to large sheets of butcher paper.*

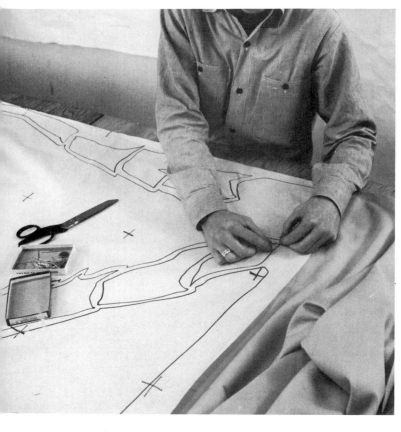

Warrior Ant: Step 3. *Next Ball pins the full-scale drawing to the appliqué fabric.*

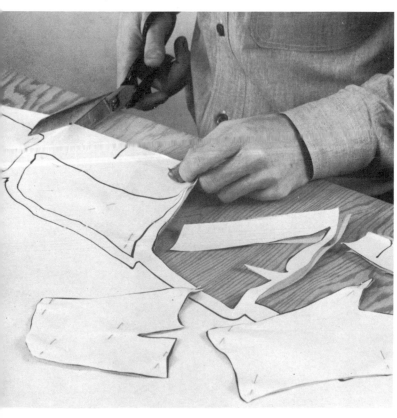

Warrior Ant: Step 4. *Then he cuts out the various shapes.*

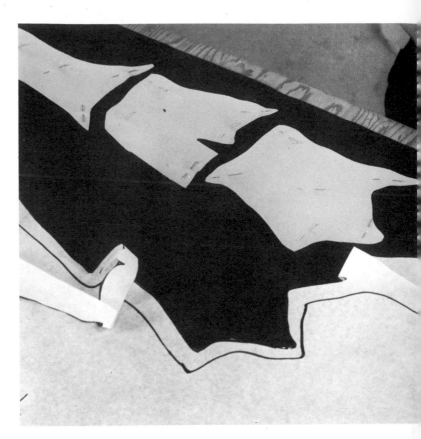

Warrior Ant: Step 5. *When all the shapes have been cut out, Ball pins them to the ground fabric. He uses the uncut portions of his full-scale drawing as a placement guide.*

Warrior Ant: Step 6. *Ball doesn't turn under the edges of the appliqué pieces. He machine stitches them to the ground fabric using a tight zigzag stitch that securely binds the edges.*

Warrior Ant *by Ted Ball. Medium-weight cotton sail cloth, 6' x 12'. Collection of the Natural History Museum of Los Angeles. Ted Ball's bold interpretation of the warrior ant reared up in attack position is one in a series of pieces he is doing on the various disciplines of science.*

Sun, Birds, and Tree *by Gonzalo Duran. Cotton and wool, 20½" x 60½". Photo courtesy of Zachary Waller Gallery, Los Angeles. This is an interpretation of the life-giving qualities of the sun. The pieces are machine stitched.*

Iguana *by Lucile Brokaw. Framed wool on linen, 35½" x 16½". To create a rough textural effect, the artist puckered the lizard's body and the surrounding ground fabric and attached frayed scraps of cloth, representing the spine, down the center of the lizard's back. The eyes, feet, and nails are embroidered with wool yarn.*

Porcupine Man *(Right) by Lucile Brokaw. Wool and cotton upholstery fabric, 63" x 47". Pheasant feathers and porcupine quills, as well as embroidery work, enhance the bold tactile quality of the piece. The eyes and nose are wood, attached from the back of the piece. To hang the piece, a brass rod with finials on each end was slipped through the hem at the top.*

Leo *by Lucile Brokaw. Wool on linen, 50" x 61½". The top of the lion's mane is formed from the tails of badminton birdies. The lion's tusks are taken from a necklace. The nose is embroidered with gold thread. The hands pointing toward the sun are a design element.*

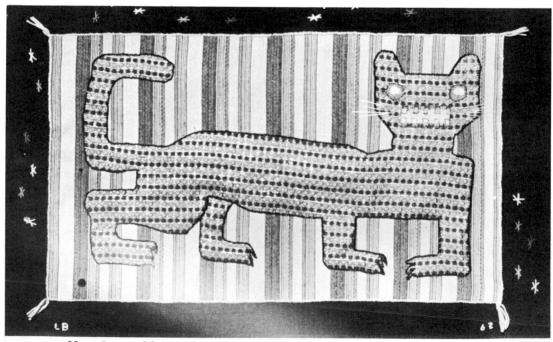

Moon Leopard *by Lucile Brokaw. Wool, cotton, and upholstery fabric mounted on wool and linen stretched over thin plywood, 27½" x 42". The upholstery fabric contains a metallic silver thread. The whiskers are strips of fiberglass.*

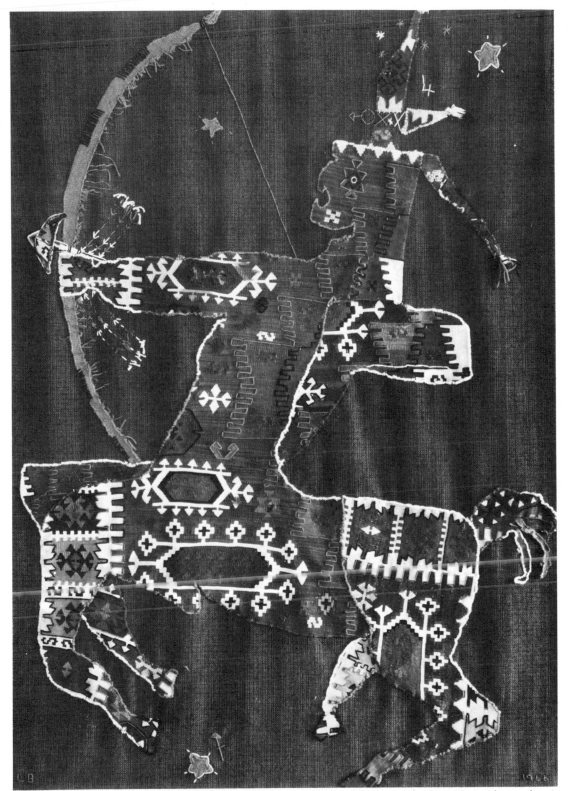

Sagittarius *by Lucile Brokaw. Wool rug on wool suiting ground, 78" x 52½". The appliqué shapes were cut from worn Indian rugs. The artist embroidered over the rugs for emphasis and added embroidered details on the ground fabric. The piece is looped and tacked over a wood rod for hanging.*

Owl by Gonzalo Duran. Wool and cotton appliqué on wool ground, 50" x 44½". Photo courtesy of Zachary Waller Gallery, Los Angeles. Much of the texture in this piece is suggested by the patterns on the fabric.

Owl Saying Goodby, But He Isn't Going to Go by Diantha Fielding. Cotton percale stretched over ¼" tempered Masonite, 30" x 40". Most of the surface of the owl is covered with embroidery in wool and cotton floss using a number of stitches. The embroidery gives a rich textural quality to the piece.

Sun Buffalo by Lucile Brokaw. Wool, cotton, and leather on heavy linen, 64" x 69½". Collection of Spa Hotel, Palm Springs. The leather body of the buffalo is attached to the ground fabric so that folds are created in the leather to give a three-dimensional effect. The artist attached strands of wool yarn in the center and left the strands hanging loose to form a shaggy mane for the head and shoulders.

Taurus (Above) by Lucile Brokaw. Wool on upholstery linen and wool, 65½" x 56". The body
of the bull was cut from a worn Indian rug. The
leaves on the branches were cut from thin
sheets of brass, and the flowers were cut freehand from wool felt. Facial details were embroidered.

Red Sun (Right) by Gonzalo Duran. Cotton and
wool, 51" x 37". Photo courtesy of Zachary
Waller Gallery, Los Angeles. Bright colors and
simple shapes create this striking design.

9
REVERSE
APPLIQUÉ

The usual method of appliqué permits the stitcher to cut shapes from any number of colored or patterned fabrics and sew them to a larger ground fabric to form a design. Reverse appliqué requires a layer of fabric for each color used in the design. It's the reverse of the usual method in that the design is created by *cutting shapes out* of the various layers to reveal a particular color. *Thus, it's a process of removing fabric shapes to form your design, rather than adding them.*

For example, suppose red, white, and blue are the desired colors. Assume that red is the top color; white's the middle layer; and blue is the bottom layer. These three pieces of fabric of equal size would be layered and basted together in the order mentioned. Where a bit of white is required in the design, you cut out the desired shape in the red top layer thus revealing the white. Where blue is required, you cut the shape from the red top layer and the middle white layer to allow the blue to show. The edges of each cutout shape must be turned under and stitched down. The result is a richly textured surface with a padded, carved quality; and in the sense that you're cutting away material to form a design, you're actually carving.

CRAFT OF THE SAN BLAS INDIANS

This reverse appliqué technique has been carried to a high level of artistry by the Indians of Panama's remote San Blas Islands. Working with layers of cloth in bright, tropical colors, the women of the Cuña region create their own distinctive designs. Traditionally, finished pieces of reverse appliqué work become the front and back panels of their yoked, short-sleeved blouses, which are called molas. More recently these beautiful examples of handwork have been made available for sale and export. In the United States these reverse appliqué panels are used primarily as framed or unframed wall hangings and decorative cushion covers.

TECHNICAL DIFFERENCES

Since this technique is the reverse of the usual method of appliqué, you'll find it time well invested to do a little experimenting. First, work out a simple design

Purse and Belt. *Collection of the Consulate General of Panama in Los Angeles. These have been made from reverse appliqué panels done by the San Blas Indians.*

Reverse Appliqué Panel. *Collection of the Consulate General of Panama in Los Angeles. Colorful reverse appliqué panels of great complexity are done by the Indians of Panama's San Blas Islands.*

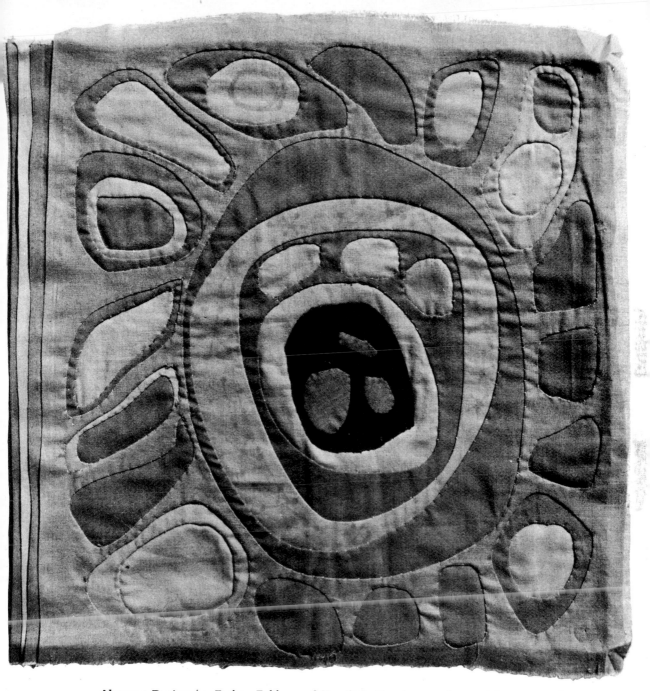

Abstract Design *by Esther Feldman. 24" x 36". Five layers of material were used to create this abstract design. It has not yet been mounted.*

Bird Hotpad *by Esther Feldman. Cotton percale, washable and color fast. Details are added by embroidery. Since reverse appliqué requires several layers of material, the piece does not require stuffing or a lining.*

on paper. Then, do a small, easy-to-handle practice piece—say 8" or 10" square—to get the feel of the technique. You'll learn that you won't be able to make your shapes as geometrically precise as in traditional, applied work. Also the turnunder will be narrower than what you're accustomed to using in applied work. Remember too that applied shapes are cut larger than the desired finished size to allow for their turnunders. However, since you're working in reverse, you'll cut the shapes smaller than the desired finished size because the turnunder will increase rather than decrease their size.

SELECTING THE FABRIC

The number of layers you'll need is determined by the number of colors in your design. Lightweight cotton with a close, even weave, such as percale, is best for this technique. Heavy fabrics are too bulky, and loosely woven material is impossible. Plan to use only two to five layers; more layers than that become difficult to handle.

Cut the fabric layers 2" or 3" larger than the desired finished size to allow for hemming and a certain amount of pulling in that occurs when you work. It's easy to keep track of the colors if you graduate the size of the layers at one edge so that the different layers can be seen.

TRACING AND BASTING

With a soft lead pencil, draw the shapes that are to be cut from the top layer onto the fabric. Baste the layers of fabric together in a loose grid starting from the center, then around the outer edges. This basting holds the layers in place while you work. You'll cut some of the basting threads when you snip out your shapes, but enough will remain in place to be effective.

CUTTING OUT AND TURNING UNDER

Use small, sharply pointed scissors. Poke the point of the scissors through the top layer of fabric and cut away the design shapes you drew in with pencil. Turn under the raw edges of the cutout shapes. Sew these edges down using a double

thread that matches the color of the fabric. You may find it helpful to pin the edges of the cutout shape under before you begin sewing, but you can simply turn the edges under as you sew. Use the slip stitch or the running stitch. Let your stitches go through to the back of the bottom layer so that all the fabric layers are held securely in place. Where necessary, clip the curves and sharp points to make them lie flat, just as you'd do in applied work.

When you cut away several layers to reveal a particular color, you needn't hem each layer separately because the hem of the top layer will conceal the raw edges of the underlying layers. If possible, cut back the edges of the underlying layers to eliminate bulkiness.

Continue drawing your design shapes, cutting, and sewing each layer except the bottom one, which must remain uncut to serve as a background.

PATCHING UP A MISTAKE

If you cut away an underlying area of color you didn't intend to, don't despair. Simply insert a scrap of fabric, slightly larger than the cutout area, into the opening. Turn under the raw edges of the upper layer and sew them down, making sure your stitches go through the inserted scrap. The same method can be used if you decide to add additional colors to a piece.

For variation, you can combine the reverse and applied techniques. For instance, you can turn under the edges of a cutout shape and applique it right back into the opening from which it was cut. This leaves a border of contrasting color around the shape. And, of course, you can always embellish a finished piece with touches of embroidery.

REVERSE APPLIQUÉ OWL

The following directions will serve as a general guide for your own reverse appliqué work. The finished size of the owl is 36" x 44".

MATERIALS

1. Butcher paper

2. Cotton percale, a different color for each of the five layers.

3. Sewing needles.

4. Sewing thread.

5. Embroidery thread.

ASSEMBLING THE DESIGN AND THE FABRIC LAYERS

1. Work out your design on butcher paper; then make a tracing of the original design on a second piece of butcher paper. Cut out the various shapes of the design from this tracing to use as patterns.

2. This owl is composed of five layers of fabric designated A, B, C, D, and E. To help keep track of the colors of the various layers, cut and arrange the layers in graduated sizes so that the color of each layer is shown at the top of the piece. See the diagram on the opposite page.

3. Baste together the layers of fabric in a loose grid starting from the center. Also baste around the edges to hold the layers in place.

CUTTING AND APPLIQUÉING

4. With a soft pencil, transfer the large wing shape, underbody, and top of the owl's head onto layer A.

5. Cut out these parts of the owl from layer A, revealing the color of layer B.

6. Next, transfer the feet and beak shapes to layer A. These shapes are cut away from layers A and B to reveal layer C. Trace the small wing shapes onto layer B and cut away to reveal layer C. Also transfer the two teardrop shapes, which delineate the eye area, onto layer A and cut through layers A, B, and C to reveal layer D.

7. Next, trace the eyes onto layer D and cut them out to reveal layer E. Also trace the owl's talons onto layer A and cut through the layers to reveal layer E.

8. Complete all the hemming around the various cut-out shapes. Then with embroidery add the details such as the heavy lines around the wings and lower body as well as the feathers on the owl's breast.

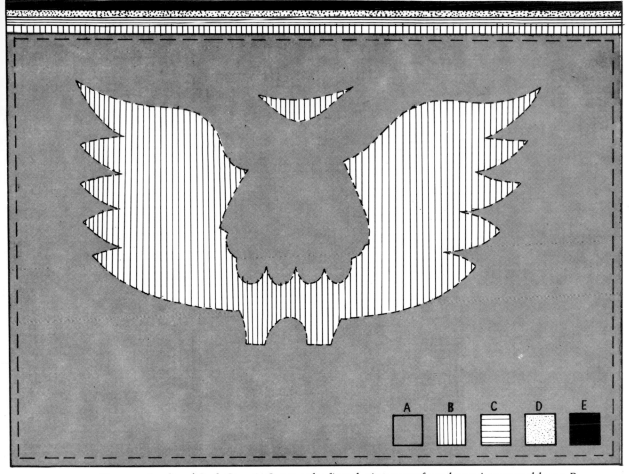

Reverse Appliqué Owl: Step 1. *Cut out the first design parts from layer A to reveal layer B.*

Reverse Appliqué Owl: Step 2. *The feet, beak, and small wings are cut out to reveal layer C; the background of the eyes is cut to reveal layer D.*

Reverse Appliqué Owl: Step 3. *The eyes and talons are cut out to reveal layer E.*

Reverse Appliqué Owl: Step 4. *Embroidery adds the final details.*

Reverse Appliqué Owl *by Diantha Fielding. Cotton percale, 36" x 44". The stitching around the small wing areas and talons has not yet been done so you can see the bastings. In this piece, the appliqué pieces are being machine stitched so there's no need to turn under the cut edges.*

10
CHILDREN'S PROJECTS

Children feel comfortable with fabric and thread, familiar items in their world, and they will enjoy appliqué if the work and ideas are kept spontaneous. While even three and four year olds love to put stitches into fabric, appliqué requires a little more control, and the examples of work shown in this chapter were made by children between five and thirteen.

When you're working with children, technique and craftsmanship should not be stressed. The important thing is the opportunity appliqué offers them to explore and develop their own creative sense. Their craftsmanship will improve as they go along. Youngsters have short attention spans, and you can see their minds drifting off to more entertaining pastures if you go on about such things as uniform stitch length or planning a design to scale. They want to get on with the work, the exciting part. Don't we all?

Keep verbal instructions to a minimum. Too much instruction simply dampens their enthusiasm, and you'll find you may have their polite little bodies there but that their minds are on their new kitten or up in the tree fort. Allow them to make their own choices each step of the way, and they'll feel the work is truly theirs. They need freedom to experiment and make mistakes too and freedom to find solutions to problems as they arise. You'll be surprised how creative some of those solutions will be. The best way to help them is to let their natural enthusiasm lead them and you.

MATERIALS

Gather a bunch of fabric together and separate it into groups of solid colors, prints, and textures. You'll also need needles with large eyes (they're easier for youngsters to thread), scissors, spools of differently colored thread, and a thimble. The fabric should be easy-to-sew cotton or blends, felt, and lightweight textures. Avoid anything that is hard to handle or get a needle through or anything that frays too readily because it's too frustrating. If the child has seen appliqué then he knows what it's all about, but if he's never seen any before, show him a piece of work and tell him the cut out pieces are sewn to the background. He'll get the idea.

Sunflower Face *by Karen Keller, 9 years old. Cotton percale. This was Karen's first sewing project. After cutting and arranging the flower head on the ground fabric, Karen decided to make a face in the center instead of continuing with her initial idea of a sunflower with stems and leaves.*

Turtle *(Above) by Lisa Kimbal, 9 years old. Felt appliqué on burlap, stretched over fiberboard. Lisa's idea came from a friend's pet turtle.*

Princess *(Right) by Antonia Kimbal, 5 years old. Felt and cotton appliquéd on burlap. The idea for this subject came from a children's television program.*

Sun Face by Martha Olson, 9 years old. Cotton, bias tape, and cotton fringe on linen, 21" x 18". Martha appliquéd some of her pieces with running stitches and some with fabric glue. She first drew the appliqué shapes on the material with a soft lead pencil and then cut them out. The bias tape is used for the nose, the center of the chin, and the strips between the triangles. Fringe adds the eyebrows and beard.

DECIDING ON A PROJECT

You can help him decide on a project by mentioning some possibilities—a cushion cover for his bed, a wall hanging for his room, a Christmas decoration wall hanging, or whatever. Deciding on a project will help him determine such things as size and whether or not the finished piece should be washable. The design idea might come from something in his home environment—a kite, flower, or pet turtle; or from his imagination—a princess or house or bug. It could be related to his current studies at school, a family excursion to the zoo, or a recent field trip he took with his school class. But whatever it is, let the child make the choice. It isn't necessary to plan the design on paper first, but if he wants to draw a picture, that's fine. The kind of simplified drawing children do is just right for appliqué. You might decide to use some of his drawings as designs on your own family quilt.

CHOOSING THE FABRIC

It's important that the child be able to handle all the different fabrics, to play with one color against another, and to get the feel of the textures. If he decides to put a lavender ladybug on an orange background that's just fine. It's his bug and his project.

CHOOSING AND DEVELOPING
THE DESIGN

Let him cut the ground fabric first. That will give him an idea of the space he has to work with. Then he can cut the appliqué shapes directly from the fabric without a pattern. He'll probably arrange each shape on the ground fabric as he cuts because he's eager to see the piece take shape. Children seem to have an innate sense of design balance, and they will rearrange the shapes till they're satisfied with the effect. It's a good idea to keep his drawing, kite, or whatever nearby so he can refer to it as he cuts.

If a child is working from a drawing, don't give him the idea he has to stick to it or carry out every detail. The flower face on p. 123 started out with a drawing of a sunflower—stem, leaves, and all. While arranging the petals on the ground fabric,

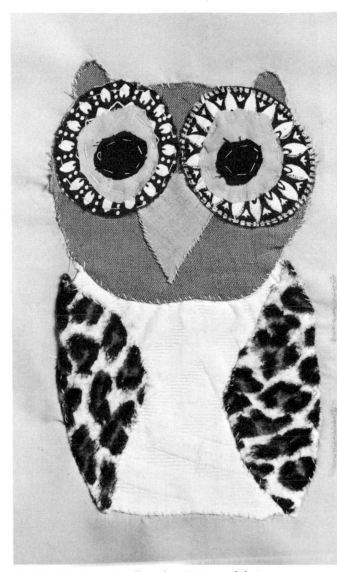

Owl *by Marianne Hollinrake. Various fabrics on cotton percale, 21" x 21". Marianne began her project by drawing pictures of various animals she likes. Then she decided on the owl, and using her drawing for a guide, she cut the motifs freehand from fabric scraps.*

The Jungle *(Above) by Lars and Lise Carver, 9 and 7 years old. Cotton and yarn, 34" x 27". In this brother-sister project, the animals were cut freehand and appliquéd with buttonhole stitches. Other embroidery stitches added details to the animals, and the lion's tail is formed from braided yarn. The children's mother backed the piece and finished the edges.*

Apple Tree *(Right) by Susan McCarthy, 13 years old. Susan cut apples from printed fabric to supply fruit for her tree. She used straight stitches, running stitches, and French knots as design elements.*

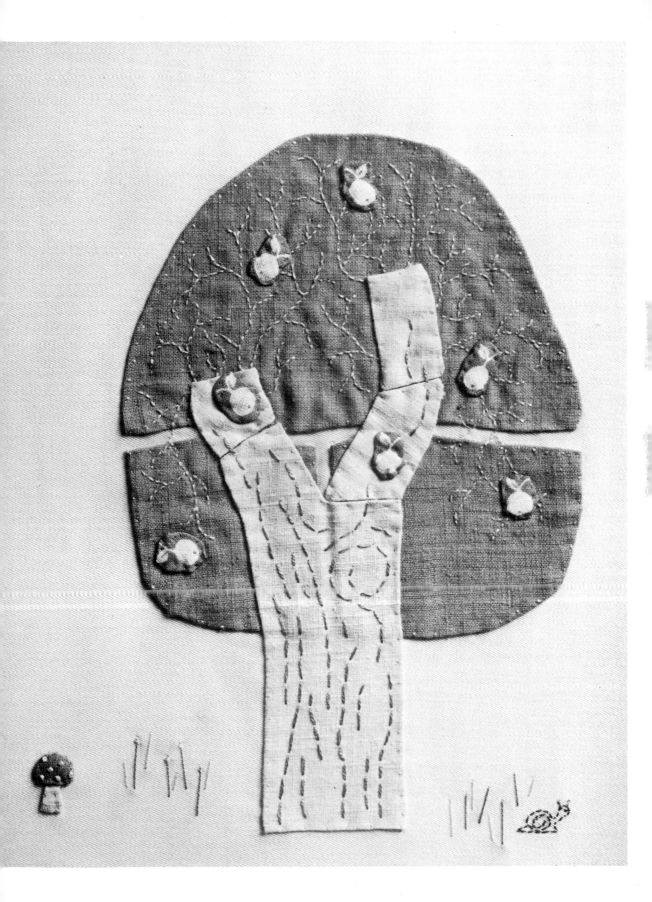

Karen decided to do just the flower head, and then later she decided to put a face in the center. Decision-making is part of the fun, and incidentally, part of the learning experience. When all the cutting is completed, put in one or two pins to show him how to pin the shapes to the ground fabric so that they stay in place while he sews.

STITCHES

Now is a good time to show your child a simple running stitch if he doesn't already know it. A double knotted thread is best because a single thread is too apt to pull out of the needle. Let him have his own needle and fabric so he can stitch right along with you while you're demonstrating on your own piece of cloth. Having his own materials helps him feel that the work is all his. When he's interested and seems to have enough control, you can show him other simple stitches, such as a buttonhole or chain stitch, and how they give a different effect on the edge of a cut out shape. Whenever a child seems bored, let him stop and pick up his work another time so that appliqué is something he looks forward to and enjoys.

Let the child choose the color of thread he wants to use, whether matching or contrasting. If he's old enough he can bring the needle up from the back so that the knot is hidden and he can end the piece with a couple of back stitches. But it's fine for very young children just to begin with the knot on top and to tie a knot with the two loose threads at the end.

TURNUNDER

Most children under ten become frustrated trying to manage a turnunder so just forget making one. Such refinements come later as their enthusiasm and pride in their work grow. Some children, however, become upset if their work doesn't look neat, or they notice that the edges on your work are turned under, and then they'll want to do the same. Explain that it's like a hem, and help them pin the turnunder if they need the help.

FINISHING THE PROJECT

When the sewing is completed, it's encouraging to your youngster if you help him complete the project so his work can be displayed. If it's a wall hanging, machine stitch a header at the top to slip a hanging rod through or he can thumbtack wood dowels at the top and bottom of the piece and tie a hanging cord at each end of the top dowel. You can stretch the work over a piece of heavy cardboard and secure it on the back with staples or masking tape. If it's a cushion cover, machine stitch a backing on and supply him with some kapok for a filler, or you may have a weary cushion that he can insert into his cover.

Pet Mouse *by Betsy Campbell, 12 years old. Cotton block for a remembrance quilt. The subject of each quilt block recalls a special family memory or things seen near Betsy's California home. When there are enough quilt blocks, they'll be sewn together to make the quilt top.*

Quilt Blocks *by Betsy Campbell, 12 years old. These are cotton blocks decorated with appliqué and embroidery which Betsy will eventually make into a remembrance quilt. The "T" is the initial of a member of Betsy's family. The ladybug and the snake are things that Betsy has seen near her home.*

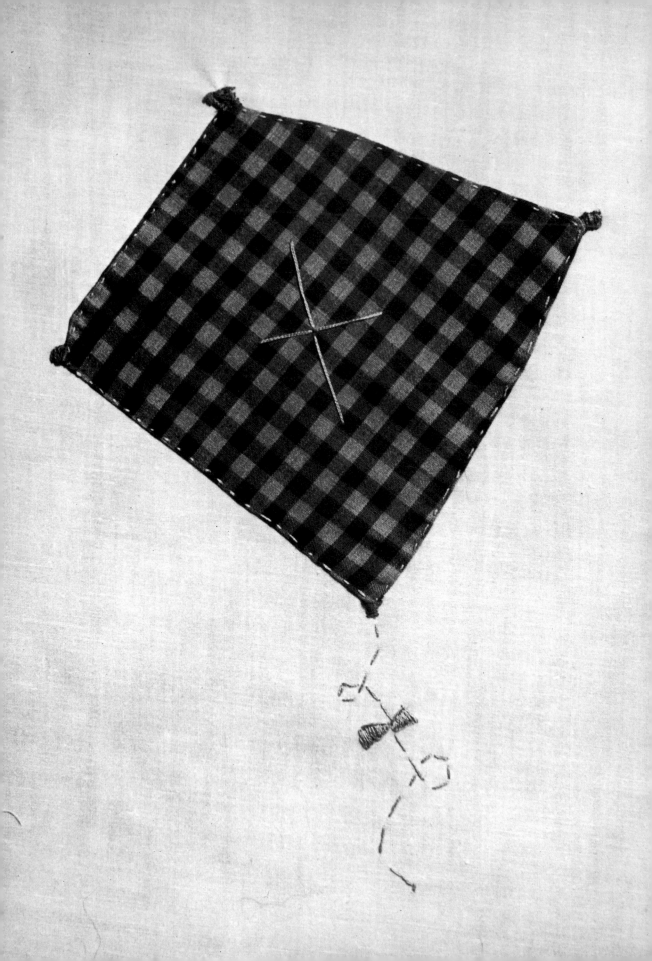

GLOSSARY

Basting. Long, loose stitches.

Batting. Slightly matted sheets or rolls of carded cotton or Dacron. It's used for stuffing, padding, or quilting.

Bias tape. Long lengths of material cut on the bias from a wide piece. It can be bought already prepared. It's used to bind the edges of a fabric.

Blind hemming. The sewing of hems so that the stitches do not show on the right side of the cloth; the stitches are called blind stitches.

Broadcloth. A fine, closely woven, lustrous cotton or polyester/cotton fabric made in a plain weave. It's widely used for apparel, such as shirts or dresses.

Burlap. Called hessian in U.K.

Butcher paper. Greaseproof paper.

Cotton perle. A loosely twisted, mercerized cotton thread with a rope or cordlike appearance. It's principally used for needlework. Also called pearl cotton.

Denim. A strong, serviceable, yarn-dyed cotton fabric, commonly in blue or brown. The heavier weight is used for overalls and work clothes while the lighter weight is used for sports clothes.

Dressmaker pins. Fine quality straight pins made with slender shafts.

Dressmaker shears. Scissors with specially shaped handles and blades so that the material can be cut without lifting it.

Drill. A strong, twilled, cotton fabric, medium to heavy in weight. It resembles denim and is used for work clothes and uniforms.

Duck. Any of a large group of strong, firm, plainly woven fabrics. While usually made of cotton, linen is sometimes used.

Embroidery needles. Needles which have larger eyes for ease in threading.

Embroidery shears. Small scissors with small, well-pointed tips for ease in working with embroidery thread and stitches.

Even-weave fabric. Fabric that has been plainly woven, that is, not in a twill or satin weave.

Eyelet. A dress fabric characterized by cut-out areas or figures that have stitching around them.

Kite by Betsy Campbell, 12 years old. Cotton block for a remembrance quilt.

Felt. Although felt can mean a non-woven material of wool, hair, fur, or man-made products, appliqué normally uses cotton felt, a woven fabric that is either napped on both sides and pressed or just pressed. It resists raveling but it's not washable.

Finial. An ornamental termination of a rod.

Finishing edges. Hemming or binding the edges of fabric to prevent raveling.

Finish of material. All processes through which fabric passes after being taken from the loom. This includes such things as bleaching, dyeing, and sizing.

Floss. Loosely twisted, lustrous embroidery thread.

Frontpiece. The top of a quilt or other similar article with multiple layers. The layer which carries the design.

Ground fabric. Fabric which will form the background of an appliqué piece. The appliqué shapes are attached to the ground fabric.

Hard finish fabric. A fabric, usually cotton, woolen, or linen, which is finished without a nap.

Interlining. A fabric which is placed between the top and bottom layers of a multiple-layered piece, such as a quilt.

Kapok. A light fiber obtained from the seed pods of the Kapok tree. It's moisture resistant, resilient, and buoyant and is used as stuffing in pillows, mattresses, and life preservers.

Kettle cloth. A textured fabric in a cotton-Dacron blend.

Masonite. A kind of fiberboard made from pressed wood fibers.

Mercerized cotten thread. A cotton thread that has been treated with caustic soda to give it strength and luster and allow it to take dye more easily.

Mitering corners. Folding points or corners of appliqué shape to form a sharp angle.

Muslin. A large group of plainly woven cottens which are used for underwear, shirts, dresses, sheets, and pillow cases.

Nap. A fuzzy or downy surface covering one or both sides of a fabric, such as flannel.

Open heading. An open heading is a way of finishing the top of a wall hanging. The top of the banner is folded back to make an opening large enough to contain a rod, then stitched.

Percale. A plainly woven, lightweight cotton fabric. Strong and usually having a smooth, dull finish, it's used for dresses, shirts, pajamas, and similar articles.

Paste-up banner. A banner that is appliquéd using glue, instead of stitches. Although it's faster to make and can utilize more types of materials, it isn't as durable as appliqué done by sewing.

Piping. A narrow piece of fabric or a cord used to finish raw edges or for decoration.

Preshrunk fabric. A fabric which has already gone through a shrinking process so that any future shrinking will be minimal.

Selvage. A narrow edge on a fabric which runs parallel to the warp. It's made of special, stronger yarns and of a closer construction than the body of the fabric.

Sheet turndown. That part of the top sheet which is normally turned down over the blanket.

Sizing. Various compounds which are applied to yarn or fabric to increase the weight and stiffness of the fabric.

Soil retardant. A chemical treatment that causes fabrics to resist soil and moisture. Some now come in spray cans and can be applied at home.

Straight of the fabric. The straight of the fabric runs parallel to the selvage edge.

Stretcher bars. A framelike device for shaping material like a wall hanging.

Tabs. Narrow strips of material that are stitched at the top of a wall hanging or banner. A supporting rod is slipped through the round opening made by the tabs.

Tacking. Individual stitches, used alone, to hold two or more pieces of fabric together.

Turnunder allowance. That part of the appliqué shape which is turned under when the piece is stitched down. Therefore, the cutout shape becomes smaller all around when it is in place on the ground fabric.

BIBLIOGRAPHY

Alexander, Eugenie,
Fabric Pictures.
London, Mills & Boon Ltd., 1963

Bager, Bertel,
Nature as Designer.
New York, Van Nostrand Reinhold, 1966,
  and London, F. Warner Co. Ltd., 1967

Brightbill, Dorothy,
Quilting as a Hobby.
New York, Sterling, 1964

Butler, Anne,
Embroidery for School Children.
Newton Centre, Mass., Branford, 1969

Carter, Jean,
Creative Play with Fabric and Threads.
New York, Taplinger, and London, B. T.
  Batsford Ltd., 1968

Colby, Averil,
Patchwork.
Newton Centre, Mass., Branford, and
  London, B. T. Batsford Ltd., 1958

————*Patchwork Quilts.*
New York, Scribner's, and London, B. T.
  Batsford Ltd., 1965

de Sausmarez, Maurice,
Basic Design: The Dynamics of Visual Form.
New York, Van Nostrand Reinhold, and
  London, Studio Vista Ltd., 1964

Dean, Beryl,
Ecclesiastical Embroidery.
Newton Centre, Mass., Branford, and
  London, B. T. Batsford Ltd., 1958

Enthoven, Jacqueline,
Stitchery for Children.
New York, Van Nostrand Reinhold, 1968

————*The Stitches of Creative Embroidery.*
New York, Van Nostrand Reinhold, and
  London, Studio Vista Ltd., 1965

Harbeson, Georgiana Brown,
American Needlework.
Santa Cruz, Calif., Bonanza Books, and
  Cambridge, Wheffer & Sons Ltd., 1938

Hedin, Solweig, and Springer, Jo,
Creative Needlework.
New York, Fawcett Publications, 1969

Howard, Constance,
Inspiration for Embroidery.
Newton Centre, Mass., Branford, and
  London, B. T. Batsford Ltd., 1967

Laliberte, Norman, and McIlhany, Sterling,
Banners and Hangings.
New York, Van Nostrand Reinhold, 1964

Lane, Rose Wilder,
*Woman's Day Book of American
  Needlework.*
New York, Simon & Schuster, 1964

Laury, Jean Ray,
Appliqué Stitchery.
New York, Van Nostrand Reinhold, 1966

Meyer, Franz Sales,
Handbook of Ornament.
New York, Dover Publications, and
  London, Constable & Co. Ltd., 1957

Risley, Christine,
Machine Embroidery.
London, Studio Vista Ltd.

Russell, Pat,
Lettering for Embroidery.
New York, Van Nostrand Reinhold, and
  London, B. T. Batsford Ltd., 1971

Short, Eirian,
Embroidery and Fabric Collage.
Metuchen, N.J., Textile Book Service, and
  London, Pitman Publishing, 1967

Thomas, Mary,
Dictionary of Embroidery Stitches.
London, Hodder & Soughton Ltd., 1934

————*Embroidery Book.*
Brooklyn, N.Y., Shalom, and London,
  Hodder & Soughton Ltd., 1936

Wotzkow, Helm,
The Art of Hand Lettering.
New York, Dover Publications, and London,
  Constable & Co. Ltd., 1968

The Complete Book of Needlework.
London, Ward Lock Ltd.

Most of the things you'll need for appliqué projects can be purchased from a local yard goods or needlecraft store. Also large department stores usually carry a wide choice of threads, fabrics, and sewing implements. Specialized items, such as Masonite and other equipment needed to display wall hangings and banners, are available at most art supply stores.

SUPPLIERS LIST

U.S. Suppliers

Alice Peterson's Needleworks,
11733 Barrington Court.,
Los Angeles, Calif.

The Friday Needlework Shop,
1260 Delaware Ave.,
Buffalo, N.Y.

Jeweled Needle
920 Nicollet Mall,
Minneapolis, Minn.

The Knittery,
2040 Union Street,
San Francisco, Calif.

Lazy Daisy,
602 E. Walnut Street,
Pasadena, Calif.

Lucy Cooper Hill,
9570 Bay Harbor Terrace,
Miami Beach, Florida

Needlecraft Shop,
13561 Ventura Blvd.,
Sherman Oaks, Calif.

Needlework,
Whaler's Wharf, Building 10-A Berth 76,
San Pedro, Calif.

Nimble Needle,
2645 San Diego Ave.,
San Diego, Calif.

The Spinning Wheel,
1612 J. Street,
Modesto, Calif.

The Stearns & Foster Co.,
Cincinnati, Ohio 45215 (For quilting needs.)

Yarn Depot,
545 Suttee Street,
San Francisco, Calif.

Yarn Tree,
101-L West 5th Ave.,
Scottsdale, Arizona

Yarncrafters Ltd.,
3146 M Street N.W.,
Georgetown, Washington, D.C.

British Suppliers

Ells & Farrier Ltd.,
5 Prince's Street,
London W1

Harrods,
Brompton Road,
London SW1

Heal & Sons,
196 Tottenham Court Road,
London W1

Liberty & Co. Ltd.,
Regent Street,
London W1

Light Leather Co. Ltd.,
16 Newman Street,
London W1

Louis Grosse,
36 Manchester Street,
London W1

Macculloch & Wallis Ltd.,
25 Dering Street,
London W1

Mace & Nairn,
89 Crane Street,
Salisbury, Wilts

The Needlewoman,
146 Regent Street,
London W1

Royal School of Needlework,
25 Prince's Gate,
London SW7

Rubans de Paris,
39a Maddox Street,
London W1

Wandbee
180 Gray's Inn Road,
London WC1